Sunset

Gardening in Containers

By the editorial staffs of
Sunset Books and Magazine

Ninth Printing January 1966

Title No. 320

Lane Magazine & Book Company

Menlo Park, California

Contents

Plants in containers play a big part in creating a warm inviting atmosphere on sunny old-brick terrace.

WHY GROW PLANTS IN CONTAINERS?

When you talk to people about growing plants in containers, you become aware that during the last few years, a whole new concept of gardening has come along. Much of this, of course, has happened because today's architecture in both house and garden creates innumerable situations and backgrounds for plant displays.

But this is only one side of the coin. There's another, more basic reason for the tremendous increase in container gardening. Every true gardener has an urge to discover plants; to get to know them better by seeing them close-up, by looking at them from this angle or that, by studying their structure, texture, color, or seasonal changes.

When you isolate a plant in a container, you discover things that you never saw before when it lived among a mass of other plants.

A container garden never is monotonous. Plants can be changed to suit the seasons, arranged and combined according to colors of flowers or foliage, moved from one exposure to another. For all types of gardeners, it's an ideal method of producing quick changes in color. It's a practical way to keep a smooth succession of color coming on, and it avoids the usual feast or famine.

You can try out new plants—one or a few at a time—in boxes or tubs before you set them out in the garden.

If yours is a new garden, container plants can provide an immediate effect. A little tree covered with blossoms, pots of bulbs and annuals blooming underneath—and there is your first spring garden!

Indoor plants can skip the seasons entirely. Many are green and growing all year.

Collection of home-grown bonsai prompts design of patio and contributes graceful backdrop for outdoor living.

More work? Or less?

To some, container gardening may sound like more work, but many discover that the reverse often is the case.

When plants are concentrated in an area close at hand, they are more easily controlled as far as watering, fertilizing, weeding, and other maintenance jobs are concerned.

If you're working with bulbs, containers get around the gopher problem and solve the question of what to do with bulbs after bloom is past and foliage becomes yellow and unsightly.

If your soil is so heavy and water-logged that you can't dig or plant in it until late in spring, boxes and pots offer color without the necessity of setting out plants in the ground. In cold climates, the boxes and pots can be planted early and kept in a protected place until time to put them on display.

Checklist on container gardening

Here are the basic points that distinguish gardening with containers from other forms of garden practice:

Small patio enlivened by use of pots, plant boxes attached to fence. Pots may be removed when bloom ceases.

Daffodils, azalea give spring color on small deck outside window. Display changes with season. Plants grow in containers, sunk in boxes filled with peat moss. Background screen covered with protective plastic cloth.

1. Container plants require more frequent watering than the same plants in the garden.

2. Soil in containers needs renewal. Many plants can live for years in one soil mixture, enriched from time to time; but usually smaller-sized containers are likely to become exhausted of their nutrients after one or two seasons. You can add nutrients, but the soil itself should be renewed after a time. However, the plant will tell you when it has run through the soil; watch it rather than the calendar.

3. Because of their exposure, container plants are more sensitive to extreme heat or cold than plants in garden soil. However, they can be shifted to a protected spot.

4. Plants grown in pots, tubs, and boxes are subject to most of the same diseases and pests as their counterparts in the garden, and they are doctored with the same insecticides. However, diseased plants in containers can usually be isolated from their companions for treatment, thereby avoiding spread of infection or infestation.

5. Most container plants do best in a potting mix that is fairly light and nutritious. See the section on potting mixes.

6. Prime requirement for any container soil is adequate drainage. Plants need drained soil in varying degrees of porosity; most require rapid draining, or what is usually referred to as perfect drainage; others can take slower draining; but none will survive in heavy, gummy soil.

7. Most plants do not thrive when pot-bound. Keep them in proper-sized containers. Move them along to the next size or trim roots if they jam the container. Of course, some plants will live happily for years in the same container—notably the geranium.

8. On the other hand, plants will also suffer if placed in too large a container. The plant may get too much water which would rot the roots; or the water may flow rapidly around the outside of the root ball and through the porous soil mix rather than the root ball. The roots will not have a chance to penetrate the soil, and the plant may dry out.

9. Many patio plants can be brought indoors to extend their blooming period.

Indoor plants

Indoor plants and their culture are covered in a separate chapter elsewhere in this book.

Eight by 32-inch boxes hold variegated geraniums; 8 by 16-inch, other geraniums. The boxes could be attached on wall in this same pattern. The arrangement would work out well on the edge of a roof top, porch, deck.

Changeable pot display along entry walk provides almost all-year color. White marguerites are in 10-inch pots which slip into circular holes cut in 1 by 12-inch redwood and are held suspended by pot lip.

ERNEST BRAUN

Japanese porcelain urns — with patterns of blue and white and a touch of red — add elegant touch on second-story deck. Junipers growing in wooden buckets set on blocks of wood inside the containers to provide air and drainage space between bottom of bucket and urn. Stands hold urns off floor of deck.

CONTAINERS: HALF THE FUN, HALF THE PICTURE— SO CHOOSE THEM WISELY

You can take your pick of conventional containers or let your imagination go—the field is wide open. In photographs on these pages you see a fair cross-section of the containers available to the pot gardener. In addition to the usual pots, tubs, and boxes, there are more unusual braziers, urns, kettles, and ceramic, concrete, or iron bowls. You will even find plants growing in hollowed-out logs and volcanic rock. Always the important thing is that the container and the plant complement each other.

Following are the containers most generally available:

CLAY POTS

Flower pots are obtainable in a variety of materials and sizes.

The hundred-year monopoly of the garden by the earth-colored, *unglazed* flower pot has been challenged for several years by *glazed* pots. Both varieties have their advantages and disadvantages. The unglazed pot has very good drainage, but it dries out rapidly, particularly in hot weather, and requires more frequent watering. Though most glazed pots have drainage holes, water does not evaporate from the pot's glassy surface, and so they don't need watering as often.

Glazed pots are sold in white and many colors. Judiciously chosen, these pots can contribute a bright accent to the patio or garden corner. Chief problem is in selecting colors that do not compete or clash with the flowers or overwhelm them with greater intensity. Pastel-colored pots mingle pleasantly with the plants they hold. Gardeners who favor the unglazed pot contend that its simple and earthy color blends inconspicuously with *anything* you care to put in it.

Sizes: Pots are obtainable in a wide variety of sizes. The "standard" pot is the one most generally used. "Standard" means that it is as wide at the top as it is high, for example 2½ inches wide by 2½ inches high. Pots come in sizes beginning with 2 inches wide (called

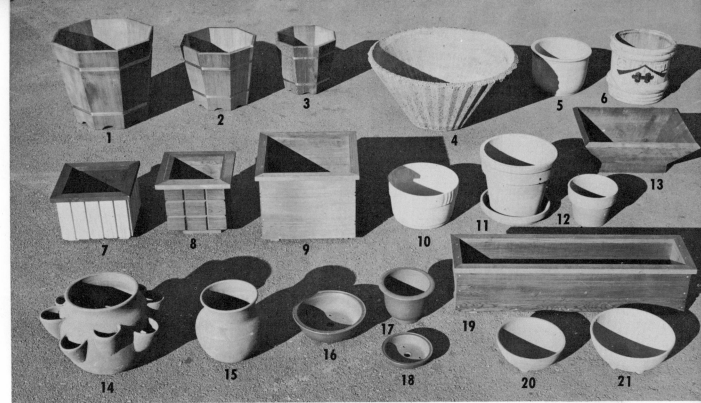

(1.) Hexagonal tub, 18 inches across, 15 deep. (2.) Same 14 by 11 inches. (3.) Same, 12 by 9¾ inches. (4.) Concrete tub 30-inch diameter, 14½ inches deep. (5.) Glazed pot 12-inch diameter, 8¾ inches deep. (6.) Soy tub, 14-inch diameter, 11 inches deep. (7.) Gray and black-stained box 13-inch square, 7½ inches deep. (8.) Capped redwood, 8½ inches square. (9.) Redwood, 18-inch square, 15 inches deep. (10.) Clay hanging pot, 13½-inch diameter, 7 inches deep.

(11.) 12-inch pot and saucer. (12.) 8-inch azalea (¾) pot. (13.) Redwood box 22 by 17 inches. (14.) Strawberry jar, 11½-inch diameter, 11 inches deep. (15.) Mexican olla, 10 inches deep, 9-inch diameter. (16.) Brown pottery, 11-inch diameter, 3½ inches deep. (17.) Same as 16, 9-inch diameter, 7 inches deep. (18.) Same, 7-inch diameter, 1½ inches deep. (19.) Redwood box, 35 by 9 inches. (20.) Clay 3-legged pot, 9-inch diameter, 4 inches deep. (21.) Same 11-inch diameter.

"thumb pots") and running up to 14 and 16 inches wide.

The containers known as "pans" are half as tall as they are wide and usually begin with the 5-inch size. Azalea and three-quarter pots are also wider than they are tall; both are three-quarters as high as they are across, that is, 6 inches across and 4½ inches high. Because of their wider base, they are more stable than the standard pots.

PLANT TUBS

Perhaps no one small piece of garden equipment can be of greater use, or do more to set a garden apart from the ordinary, than planting tubs. For small plants, of course, clay pots are wholly satisfactory, but in larger sizes, pots, whether glazed or unglazed, have the disadvantage of

---

You can find pots in many shapes and sizes. Simplest forms are always satisfying and compatible with plants. Clay pots take on soft, earthy color after long use.

weight. So, for larger flower plantings, miniature gardens, shrubs, and particularly for small trees, wooden tubs offer a high degree of utility.

Requirements

The primary requisite of such tubs is, of course, that they should be able to withstand intermittent watering

Clay pots, 18-inch diameter, set in platforms on windy deck. Conifers removed in spring, heeled-in, replaced with hydrangeas in summer.

Freesias grow well in containers. A dozen bulbs will just about fill a 7-inch pot.

Pots against posts. Geraniums — familiar, colorful, unostentatious — among the easiest potted plants to grow and care for.

LEFT. Bronze phormium in tall 14-inch pot. Hawaiian garden torch adds interest.

Irregular and windswept Shore pine in perfect scale with the squat, shiny, brown, glazed pottery jug.

A variation of the strawberry barrel, this jar holds echeveria, Aeonium caespitosum, spilling over edge.

Massive container is made of a mixture of concrete, haydite, and perlite. Handmade and hand-tamped, with cement color added; sealed on the inside with a cement.

Sturdy wooden tubs contain aralias, pruned to standard form to produce tropical, yet formal effect. Boxes made of 2 by 12-inch redwood, with design in grain.

and drying out. They must also be resistant to decay. A third requisite is that they should be so designed as to hold moisture without too-rapid drainage. In one point in particular, tubs of wood excel plant containers of any other material. Due to the insulation value of wood, even in the hot sun, heat penetrates the wood slowly, hence the roots are not likely to be scorched.

Depending upon the availability of the material in various localities, there are three kinds of wood which will meet the requirements for wooden tubs: redwood, cedar, or cypress. In some localities, it may be possible also to use wood of the black locust, osage orange, or chestnut. None of these woods requires preservative treatment.

The design of the tub should be such that joints will remain tight to prevent excess moisture losses. Holes should be provided in the bottom to facilitate drainage. The bottom of the tub should not rest directly on the ground but should be raised somewhat with legs, blocks, or cleats.

Shape and size

No hard and fast rules can be made regarding proper proportions for tubs or the kinds of plants that should be grown in them. But unless a tub is well proportioned and carefully constructed, there is hardly any point in wasting a plant in it. By the same token, a handsome container deserves a distinctive plant.

Roughly, let the general shape of the plant at maturity determine the shape of the tub or box. A squarish form is appropriate for low, bushy contours. The gardenia, Meyer lemon, Rangpur lime, and azalea appear to advantage here. A tall tub is suitable for tapering conifers such as yew and false cypresses, or broad-leafed evergreens such as boxwood. A low, squatty tub is good for plants which form a sphere of foliage on a rodlike stem, such as standard roses and fuchsias, Grecian laurel, kumquat, and others.

Ground covers are often grown at the bases of tall-stemmed, standard plants. A low planting softens the harsh line formed by the rim of the box or tub and serves as a transition between the higher plants and the containers.

Remember that plant boxes must be deep enough to allow sufficient root growth. Lantana, azalea, gardenia, and bouvardia require 12 to 18 inches. Eighteen to 24 inches are needed for camellia, rhododendron, viburnum, kumquat, laurel, and boxwood.

CONTAINERS   9

Stained, grooved redwood box 12¾ inches square, 8 deep. Liner: half

of 5-gallon can dipped in asphalt paint. Japanese maple, sedum.

THEODORE OSMUNDSON

Hydrangea in small triangular plant box, just fits into the corner.

Long handles extending from sides of planters make easy two-man lift.

This contemporary black plastic container has wrought iron stand.

Old copper cooking kettle, 28 inches across, holds a large potted aspidistra. Mainstay of pot gardens a century ago, aspidistras are hardy, nearly indestructible.

Kegs and barrels

The barrel, and its various relatives, is the Old Reliable container for shrubs and trees.

Attractive plant tubs of this type are marketed through nurseries. Some of them are made in the same dimensions as the largest ceramic tubs. They range from 8 inches "square" (8-inch diameter, 8-inch height) to 18 inches square. Some are constructed of rot-resistant wood and are usually banded with non-corrosive hoops.

If you have access to commercial barrels or kegs (a barrel has a capacity of over 32 gallons; half-barrel, 25–31 gallons; a keg, less than 25 gallons), here are some pointers about converting them to plant tubs:

1. In garden use, barrels made to hold liquids will outlast those made to hold dry materials and they are less likely to leak. You can tell them from "dry" barrels by their thicker walls.

2. Painting the inside of a barrel with a preservative paint or asphalt compound will probably extend the life of the wood, but the staves are less likely to give way than the hoops. Probabilities are that the hoop will rust out long before the wood decays.

3. Barrels last longer if kept filled and uniformly damp.

4. Weakest point in barrel construction is the joint where the lid (or bottom) fits into the staves. For this

1 GAL. KIT — 7"
5 GAL. KIT — 12"
KEGS — 1 QT. 6" — ½ GAL. 7½" — 1 GAL. 8½"
2½ GAL. KEG — 13"
5 GAL. KEG — 15½"
32 GALLON HALF-BARREL — 29"
50 GALLON BARREL — 33"
16 GAL. KEG — 23"
10 GAL. KEG — 21"

ERNEST BRAUN

Cooper displays the products of his craft: a barrel, a half-barrel, seven kegs, two kits. Fine plant tubs.

reason, do not support the full weight on rim of the barrel. Attach a cleat to the bottom that is thick enough to raise the rim of the barrel above the ground as shown in the drawing. The full weight of the dirt is then borne by the bottom, not the sides.

WEAK POINT
SAW MARK
PENCIL
SUPPORT ON CLEATS.. NOT RIM.

5. Cutting a barrel down to more usable size is tricky. Mark your line for sawing by holding a pencil rigidly against the barrel and turning the latter until the line runs all the way around it (see drawing). Cut with a hand saw, preferably a coping saw so you can cut one stave at a time.

6. Barrel capacity is rated in liquid measure. To convert gallons to dry measure, multiply gallonage by .1337. This will give you cubic feet.

Handsome Japanese maple growing in barrel cut down to three-quarters size, ample for several years' growth.

CONTAINERS 11

ROBERT COX

Sturdy oblong box 30 by 60 inches, is of redwood and combed marine plywood. Plants are blue agapanthus.

Plant box, 2 feet square at top, planted with 10 Shasta strawberry plants in January, yielded berries in May.

ABOVE. *Triangular, square boxes of geraniums form patio design.* **BELOW.** *Portable units of 1-by-8 redwood, fit inside larger boxes made of a core of 1-inch stock, trimmed on the outside with battens evenly spaced.*

BOXES

Large, square boxes have long been in favor for use with shrubs and trees. Their rectangular lines harmonize architecturally with modern house and landscape design.

Suggested proportions for a low box are these inside dimensions: width, 14, 16, or 18 inches square to height, 13, 14, or 15 inches. A 7 to 5 ratio of width to height is also suitable for this type of box.

Pleasing proportions for a tall box are 4 to 3, the sides 1/3 taller than wide. For example, if a box is 16 inches tall, it should be 12 inches wide.

For boxes less than 18 inches to a side, use 1-inch stock. For larger ones, use 2-inch stock. Always nail the bottom inside the end and sides so that the nails will help support the bottom and prevent the sides from pulling away when the loaded box is moved.

Nail 1- by 3-inch cleats across the bottom, 1/2 inch from the outside edge to keep the box off the ground.

Drainage

Bore five 1/2-inch holes per square foot in the bottom of the tub for drainage. A layer of coarse gravel in the bottom will keep dirt from clogging the holes.

LEFT. *Black clay hanging pot from Oaxaca has many drain holes. It is 6 inches high, costs equivalent of 10 cents.* CENTER. *Circular hanging container of plastic* *holds variegated nepeta.* RIGHT. *Wire basket is classic container for shade-loving plants. First, line basket with sphagnum moss or osmunda; then fill with mix.*

HANGING CONTAINERS

Hanging containers put foliage and blossoms at eye level and offer more planting room in a limited space. But more than that, hanging masses of flowers give a luxuriant look to patios, walls, and fences.

Fuchsias, tuberous begonias, and ivy geraniums are top favorites for hanging containers. But there are other possibilities. All you need is a plant that trails naturally, has attractive blossoms, and thrifty, interesting foliage. Seeds of many such plants, lobelia and balcony petunias, for example, can be sown in flats in spring and transplanted in early summer. Trailing plants, considered nuisances in the neat bed or border, are invaluable for planting in hanging pots.

Although hanging baskets and pots were originally intended strictly for trailing plants, almost any plant that strikes your fancy may be grown in hanging containers. Plants do fascinating things when they get up in the air. Some that are sedate and conventional on the ground—such as the camellia and azalea—become quite acrobatic. Branches that ordinarily grow upward will curve downward but throw flowering laterals upward. Thus you get stems in a shape something like a picture hook. You are used to seeing cascade chrysanthemums perform this way—but have you ever seen *Dianthus* Old Spice, shrimp plant, and bush morning glory in a hanging pot?

Types of hanging containers

You have a choice of several kinds of hanging containers. By using wire baskets lined with sphagnum moss, you can plant on the sides as well as in the top. Plant after the lining has been set in place but before filling with soil. The most serious disadvantage of wire baskets is rapid drying out in hot weather and in warm winds. This can be partly overcome if you will put a clay pot saucer in the bottom between the moss lining and the soil. Of course, wire baskets undoubtedly are better in the shade than in the sun.

Clay hanging pots dry out less rapidly than wire baskets. If you use new ones, be sure to soak them thoroughly before planting. Baskets made of redwood or cedar slats require much the same treatment as wire baskets. First line them with sphagnum moss, or osmunda fiber, then fill with soil. These, too, dry out quite readily and are best for shaded positions.

Solid redwood or cedar boxes are among the best for tuberous begonias, fuchsias, ferns, and other plants that like moisture and a slightly acid soil. They are cool and moisture retentive. And there seems to be a more natural association between wood and the type of plants that grow in peat moss or leaf mold.

Hangers

Be sure that your hanging baskets are suspended from

Dramatic plants provide sharp accents on pot shelf just outside Sunset building. This is New Zealand flax.

substantial hooks that will hold the weight and will not pull out. Use lag-thread clothesline hooks or screw-eyes or eye bolts.

WINDOW BOXES

A flash of friendly color just outside your window, a miniature garden of herbs within reach of the kitchen dinner-getter, a fresh fragrance blowing in with the summer breezes—these are the rewards of the window box gardener.

Dimensions

Nothing lighter than inch-thick lumber should be used. This not only discourages warping, but enables the box to hold a greater weight of soil. In most instances, window boxes should not be longer than 6 feet because of the heavy weight. If 6-foot boxes are not long enough to span the window area, build two or three smaller ones to fit the required length. When planted, the final effect will be that of one long box.

Boxes should be about 9 inches deep and 12 inches wide. This allows sufficient depth for the roots of most plants and ample room for setting a generous number of plants.

In regions with severe winters, the window box should be built with one side slanted outward to permit frozen soil to expand without bursting the box.

Supports

Window boxes should be securely supported because of their weight. On an average, window boxes will weigh about 75 pounds per foot of length. Thus, a 6-foot box can weigh 450 pounds—a substantial load to hang on the side of any house.

If you were to ask a building inspector about window boxes, this is about what he would tell you:

Supports should be bolted to wall studs or fastened with lag screws. Ordinary screws or nails are not strong enough to hold a large box. Ideally, the box should be incorporated into the house design and built at the time the house is built. If it is to be added on to an existing house, make certain that you anchor it to studding. Surest way is to penetrate the surface covering of the wall and attach it inside to studs. If the supports are strong enough for you to stand on, you can be sure that they will hold a box safely.

A light window box or pot shelf may be attached to the exterior with sturdy metal brackets, but make certain that the supports bear against studs and attach them with lag screws. Coat the brackets and screws with a rust inhibitor before attaching and keep the metal painted. Without such precautions a disagreeable streak will develop on the wall after the metal starts to rust, and in time the bracket or screws may rust through and let the box fall.

The weight factor makes it doubly necessary to build substantially if the box is to be installed in a second story window. A 100-pound box of dirt, dropping from a second story, can be a formidable hazard.

Lining

Wooden window boxes should be lined with a watertight membrane to prevent their rotting and causing the house itself to rot. Ample protection may be provided by a liner of metal or three layers of roofing paper sealed in place with hot asphalt. Copper is the most durable metal. Galvanized iron will give several years' protection, but it will rust out in time. The roofing paper membrane is flexible and self-sealing—hot weather will cause the tar to melt slightly and fill in crevices and cracks.

As a further precaution, set the box an inch away from the house. This will prevent any rot that might develop from reaching the house, and if the installation is on the ground floor, it will deter termite infestation.

Drainage

Proper drainage in window boxes is essential in order to forestall root rot.

To carry off excess water, window boxes should have 2 holes for each square foot of flooring. A 1-inch pad of gravel, spread over the bottom, will distribute the water and lead it to the outlets. Such a pad, however, can be omitted in shallow boxes, although the soil formula should be made sufficiently porous to allow water to permeate the box. To keep gravel or soil from running out the hole, cover the opening with pieces of broken pot.

Water dripping from a window box will discolor the wall of a house. It is important to make sure that your box is calked or soldered at the corners and seams to prevent water from seeping out along the edges of the box, and place the drain holes so their drip will not strike the wall.

If the box is built into the house, it will need pipes or tubes to carry off the water. Set the ends of the tubes far enough away from the house to prevent staining by the outfall. Clean out drainage tubes with wire every now and then, for they are prone to clog.

Window-box variations

A less bothersome way of growing plants in a window box is to set potted or canned plants inside the box in such a manner that only the foliage shows, not the individual container. If clay pots are used in this manner, they should be surrounded with peat moss or sawdust to hold moisture.

Another alternative is a pot shelf, made of a board with circular holes cut into it just large enough to hold pots. With this device, the color scheme can be changed at the whim of the gardener.

Both variations have the advantages that plants can be taken to the potting bench where they can be handled easily or they can be brought into the house when the weather turns hostile. Furthermore the staunch construction needed for a 200- or 300-pound window box is not essential for a shelf to hold 50 pounds of potted plants.

Landscape Architect Kathryn Imlay Stedman designed the device you see on this page for her own garden. It's made of ¼-inch angle iron welded into an open frame 12 inches wide and 10 feet long. One end is attached to a post of the carport; the other rests on a large planting box. The frame is 18 inches above the ground and 2 feet from the house (see photographs). There are 2 sets of boxes that may be interchanged on the rack, or used together as shown in the center photograph. All the boxes are 12 inches wide (the width of the rack), but one set is lower and longer than the other to give more interest to the display.

The front of the house faces north and is too shady for most plants, so they are brought along to blooming

BASIC ... *boxes of evergreen Hahn's ivy*

SUMMER ... *tuberous begonias and lobelia*

AUTUMN ... *cascading chrysanthemums*

stage in a work center, then moved to the rack. In the cool shade, flowers last longer and hold their color better than in full sun.

When nothing is in bloom, boxes of Hahn's ivy fill the rack. In late winter and early spring, azaleas and cinerarias are on display. (Other plants that could be used include hyacinths, tulips, Dutch iris, and daffodils.) In summer boxes of tuberous begonias and blue lobelia are put in the rack. Cascading chrysanthemums are the showiest flowers for fall.

Although the device is primarily for color display, it has many other merits: You can walk behind it to paint the house or wash the windows; plants are raised off the ground away from pets; and you can water, spray, feed, and pluck off faded flowers with great ease.

Raw materials for a pleasant session at the potting bench: tools, pots, seeds and cuttings ready for potting up.

CONTAINER CULTURE: *IT'S EASY IF YOU FOLLOW A FEW SIMPLE RULES*

Growing plants in containers is a simple art. The successful container gardener follows only a few rules: mainly, to set the plants in a suitable potting mixture, to keep a vigilant watering schedule which will prevent their drying out, and to groom and feed them when they, rather than the calendar, let him know that they need attention.

In this chapter we summarize the basic techniques that apply to all forms of container gardening, from growing miniatures in a teacup to tending trees in tubs.

Specialized techniques required by various types of plant materials—e.g., bulbs, vines, bonsai, succulents—are discussed in the chapters on plant materials. Growing techniques for house plants are described in the section on that subject at the end of this book.

POTTING MIX

A successful potting soil should pass these tests:

1. It should contain sufficient nutrients for plant growth and development.

2. It should be easy to work, and easy for the roots to penetrate.

3. It should be sufficiently porous for water to penetrate it thoroughly, but not so open that it lets water run through too rapidly.

Only rarely does a garden loam meet these exacting requirements. Potting soil thus has to be "manufactured" to a formula. You can buy it in sacks at the nursery, or you can mix it yourself. A long-time basic formula, suitable for most containers, has been

2 parts good garden loam
1 part sand
1 part peat or equivalent

This formula is subject to endless variations, depending mainly upon the character of the loam. If plants growing in your garden are healthy and vigorous, and if your soil is easy to work, you can assume that this soil will be suitable for use in potting mixtures. But if you've noticed deficient plant growth, or if the soil compacts easily and is difficult to handle, you had better avoid using it in mixes.

At potting time, the soil mixture should be damp but not wet. A good test for dampness is the same as the standard one for soil texture: squeeze a handful hard. If it falls apart quickly when the hand is opened, it is too dry; if any water comes out, it is too wet; and if it retains its shape as squeezed and merely cracks slightly, it is damp enough.

THE U. C. POTTING MIX

In recent years, soil scientists at the University of California have worked out a soil program for container plants that is being widely followed by nurseries and can just as easily be applied to the home garden.

Although some of the ingredients required for the fertilizer portion of the formula may not be readily obtainable in some localities, we are describing this mix in detail because of the remarkably successful record that it is enjoying.

Simply, the U. C. Mix is formed around two components: a near-neutral rooting medium (sand and peat) plus tested fertilizer formulations. It is designed to avoid these common faults in container gardening:

1. Lack of good drainage and all of the troubles that follow it. Too often the tiny pores in a clay or silt soil become completely filled with water leaving no space for air. Waterlogging, even for a short period of time, stops growth, injures roots. On the other hand, the considerably larger pores in a sand and peat moss mixture cannot be fully occupied by water unless drainage is prevented. Both water and air can occupy the pore spaces of the mix. A well-aerated soil is a well-drained soil.

Most organic materials (according to U. C. research) are favorable to good aeration. If, however, these are sufficiently decomposed, a "mucky" condition may develop which is similar to clay in its ability to obstruct air movement. Leaf molds and manures reach this stage quite rapidly, as compared with peat moss or sawdust.

2. Feast and famine in nutrient supply. Mixes containing manures, composts, leaf mold, plus added fertilizers, deliver varying amounts of nutrients depending upon water and temperatures. It is impossible in such mixtures to have a constant level of fertility.

3. Excess salinity. A mix with poor permeability, bad drainage, will accumulate excess salts from irrigation water, fertilizers, manures, and leaf mold. The only safe container mix is one that can be leached—flushed out with excess water.

When camellias or rhododendrons show tip or marginal burning of leaves and partial defoliation, you have excess salt trouble. When leaf damage shows, considerable damage has already been done to the root system and recovery will be slow.

Azaleas and gardenias are most sensitive to excess salts. They show root damage by wilting of leaves or at times a spectacular collapse of the entire plant.

The build-up of harmful salts occurs in many ways: Too much fertilizer; some leaf molds are high in salts; manures from feed lots is another source; watering that wets the soil without run-off gradually builds up salt content.

With the mixture of fine sand and peat, or peat, the danger of excess soluble salts can be avoided by periodic leaching with water. To leach salts from a container, simply water double the requirement of the container. If irrigation water is of poor quality, leaching should be frequent and heavy to combat salinity.

Four basic mixes

The basis for the U. C. basic mixture is a combination of fine sand and peat moss, blended in varying proportions to meet the needs of different classes of plants and types of containers. A mixture of sand and peat approaches loam in water and nutrient retention, but avoids the complications involved where clay is present. It offers excellent drainage and is easily leached of accumulated salts.

The fine sand is technically "minus 30 and plus 270"—meaning that the grains pass a 30-mesh screen but not a 270 mesh. The peat moss supplies the organic portion. Unlike manures, leaf molds, and composts, it is of uniform and known quality. Furthermore, it is also of known low fertility, thus leaving the supply of nutrients almost wholly to the fertilizer formulas designed to go with the mix. If peat is not obtainable, other materials may be substituted, e.g., redwood sawdust, fir bark, rice hulls.

Here are four mixes and the types of plants for which they are best suited:

1. Suitable for a majority of plants. Excellent for large containers with good drainage.
Rooting medium: 50% fine sand, 50% peat moss

Fertilizer (per yard of mix):

    2½ lbs. hoof and horn or blood meal

    8 oz. potassium sulfate

    2½ lbs. single superphosphate

    7½ lbs. dolomite lime

    2½ lbs. calcium carbonate lime

2. Useful for succulents and other drought-resistant plants. Good for large boxes and tubs with adequate drainage.

Rooting medium: 75% fine sand, 25% peat moss

Fertilizer (see mix no. 3)

3. Recommended for azaleas, camellias, rhododendrons, and other acid-tolerant plants. Can be used in containers with somewhat obstructed drainage, dish gardens.

Rooting medium: 25% fine sand, 75% peat moss

Fertilizer (per yard of mix):

    2½ lbs. hoof and horn or blood meal

    8 oz. potassium sulfate

    2 lbs. single superphosphate

    5 lbs. dolomite lime

    4 lbs. calcium carbonate lime

4. Very lightweight mix. Used for azaleas, sometimes for gardenias and camellias.

Rooting medium: 100% peat moss

Fertilizer (per yard of mix):

    2½ lbs. hoof and horn or blood meal

    6 oz. potassium sulfate

    1 lb. single superphosphate

    2½ lbs. dolomite lime

    5 lbs. calcium carbonate lime

For all of the above formulas, mix the fine sand, peat, and dry ingredients thoroughly.

Follow-up fertilizings

Fertilizers for follow-up feedings start two weeks after planting. Apply a water dilution of ammonium nitrate, 1 teaspoon to a gallon, every third irrigation. After 2½ months, shift to a liquid fertilizer containing ammonium nitrate, di ammonium phosphate, and potassium chloride, at the rate of one level teaspoon of each to 2 gallons of water. Apply every third irrigation.

Alternate mix

If shopping for the above ingredients involves too much searching, or if you want to mix only enough for a few pots, do this: use perlite and peat moss—half and half. Add 1 heaping teaspoon of lime to every gallon of the peat-perlite mix. As you mix the dry ingredients, sprinkle on a commercial liquid fertilizer (one that contains nitrogen, phosphorus, potash), diluted according to directions on the label.

POTTING PLANTS

In general, sowing seeds in pots to remain there permanently without transplanting is not so satisfactory as sowing seeds and growing seedlings in flats before potting them up.

Seedlings of slow-growing material and rooted cuttings should be transferred from the seed flat or cutting box to a 2-inch flower pot and successively "potted on" into larger pots as the roots develop. Usually small transplants should be potted up a little deeper than they are in the seed flat. This places them in a firm upright position and helps them to produce stronger and more abundant roots.

Cleaning pots

It is most important to use clean pots, otherwise your plants may be bothered by fungus and mold. Soak new pots in water overnight, so that when you do your planting and water the new plant in, the water will go to the plant and not be soaked up by the new pot.

Clean old pots by scrubbing them with a stiff brush in hot soapy water to which some household bleach has been added, then rinse with plain water. Let them dry out. This will allow the bleach to evaporate so that it will not hurt the new plant material. Then soak the cleaned pots overnight as you would a new pot.

Provide drainage

When potting a transplant, first put in drainage materials, then a soft cushion of potting mixture that the tender roots of the young transplant will be able to penetrate. Set the plant in the pot on top of this cushion and fill around the edges with extra potting mixture being careful to firm the plants in well to provide as much soil as possible for the roots. Firm potting also prevents roots from filling the pot too quickly. After you place the transplant in the pot, hold it in position and carefully firm the soil around the roots to eliminate air pockets. But don't pack the soil so tightly as to form a solid mass that tender roots cannot penetrate.

Be careful to set the plant in place so it is neither too deep nor too high in the pot. If too deep, it will not have enough room for root development; if too high, its roots will not be able to fill in the pot rapidly enough to prevent sour soil.

Do not fill the pot to the rim. Leave some room between the surface of the soil and the top of the pot rim to hold water. As a rule of thumb, allow one-half of the depth of the rim.

POTTING. *Step 1: Assemble the ingredients for potting mix: loam, sand, peat moss or equivalent; or buy mix.*

Step 2. Select a proper-sized pot that has been scrubbed ahead of time, put piece of broken pot over hole.

Step 3. Cover bottom of the pot with layer of gravel or small pebbles. You may also add a pad of sphagnum.

Step 4. After planting, water thoroughly. Good method: partly immerse pot until the soil is well dampened.

After planting, water thoroughly. If water passes through rapidly, tamp the soil; if it remains on top, the soil needs loosening. Set your plants in a protected spot where they will not be exposed to strong sun or destructive dry wind. After a week or so (depending on the season) they may be gradually exposed to the weather.

POTTING-ON

When the plant has used up all the food in the pot and filled the soil space with its roots, it usually must be shifted to a larger container, or it will be stunted. (In growing bonsais, of course, you deliberately keep the plant in a small container in order to restrict growth.) The plant is ready for shifting to a larger pot when its roots show through the drainage hole or when you find, upon knocking the plant out of its pot, that the roots form a network around the outside of the earth ball.

It is easy to tip a plant out of a pot if you run a knife (preferably an old table knife) around the ball to loosen the soil. To finally remove the plant; turn it upside down, with the top of the ball in the palm of your hand. Let the plant stem come between the index and middle fingers. Then, holding the bottom of the pot with the other hand, rap the rim of the pot on the edge of a bench or any solid wooden surface. The ball of soil will slide into one hand and the pot will remain in the other. If only a few roots are visible, the plant is not ready for a shift and should be replaced in the pot, the bottom of which is then rapped on the bench to firm the ball of soil back in the pot. Never press the loosened ball back in the pot as it might break the roots. Be sure the soil is somewhat moist when a plant is knocked out.

It is important at all times to avoid putting plants in pots that are too large, but it is especially so in wet or

CLYDE CHILDRESS

POTTING-ON. *1. When the roots grow through drainage hole, this is signal that the plant is ready to be potted-on to a larger pot. Important to use only next size.*

2. Remove the plant by inverting the pot, tapping rim sharply against bench edge. If plant sticks, run knife around inside of pot. Trim matted roots before potting.

cold weather. When plants are overpotted, their roots do not occupy enough of the soil area, and as a result the soil remains damp for long periods. If this condition continues, the soil sours and root rot is liable to occur.

It is usually best to shift potted plants to pots that are only one size larger. However, with fast-growing plants, you can skip a size (for example, transfer a plant from a 4-inch pot into a 6-inch pot).

Old, pot-bound plants sometimes need "shouldering," that is, rubbing off of some of the surface soil so that the plant roots will be brought into contact with the new soil. Old roots may also be trimmed at this time.

WATERING CONTAINER PLANTS

All container plants need watering more often than the same plants in the open ground. The more extensive the root system and the more extensive the foliage growth of the plant, the more water will be needed. The root system of any plant adapts itself to a certain extent to the soil in which it finds itself and to the amount of moisture in that soil, but a potted plant, living and growing in the restricted area of its container, has to have more allowances made for it.

As each type of soil and each plant has its individual watering requirements, general rules of watering are misleading. Every gardener must experiment with his own container plants to establish their moisture requirements.

Daily watering will be in order on hot days, or even twice daily in the case of small clay pots in sunlight.

Plants in wooden containers need less watering than plants in clay pots. And plants in metal containers need even less.

Containers in groups will dry out less than those standing by themselves; the plants shade each other, and there is somewhat less circulation of warm air.

With most plants, you will have greater success if you do not keep the soil soaked to capacity. When you do water, do so thoroughly but allow enough time to elapse between waterings for the plant to take up a good portion of water in the soil. Test the soil by feeling it or by lifting the container. If the soil feels wet or if the container is comparatively heavy, there is water in the soil; if light, better give it a good soaking.

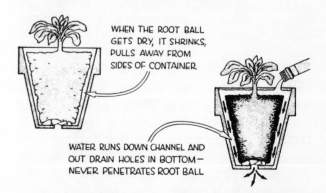

WHEN THE ROOT BALL GETS DRY, IT SHRINKS, PULLS AWAY FROM SIDES OF CONTAINER

WATER RUNS DOWN CHANNEL AND OUT DRAIN HOLES IN BOTTOM— NEVER PENETRATES ROOT BALL

However, containers are tricky. You can water one for months, literally pour water through it every day, and not saturate the soil.

3. Place a layer of potting mix over a piece of broken crock inverted over the drainage hole. Center the plant on the cushion of soil and firmly fill in all around it.

4. Firm in the soil by pressing with thumbs or a stick. Leave an inch or more space between surface of soil and top of pot for water. Water by soaking from below.

Once the soil in a container dries out, the natural course of water is through the space between the root ball and the perimeter of the container and out the drain hole in the bottom without penetrating the soil. If you turn out the soil ball in a pot, you often will find the roots wound around the outside of the ball. They are there trying to get the water that runs down the sides.

It is a wise idea when first potting your plants to make sure that the pot is well-soaked in water before filling in the potting mixture and planting the plant. Otherwise the first water you give the plant will be used to soak up the pot.

As we have pointed out, it is very important to see that your plant has enough water, but on the other hand you also have to be careful not to overwater your container plants. Soil that is saturated with water endangers plant growth. If soil is filled with water from too much watering, for too long a time, not only around the soil particles but in the air spaces between, the air will be driven from the soil and the plant will suffocate or drown.

Methods of watering

With most container plants, you can simply apply water to the soil's surface with a gentle stream from the hose or watering tube. Some gardeners prefer a long-snouted watering pot or hose-attached watering tube that can nose in under foliage.

Pots may be watered from below. You can stand the pot in a pan of water or a filled pot saucer for a few hours. Don't overdo it, however, for a prolonged bath may lead to root rot.

To bring potted plants into full water capacity so that they will take up a water supply evenly, dunk them in a tub or pail of water until the soil stops bubbling, as water takes the place of air in the structure of the soil.

Vacation watering

There are several ways to keep potted plants watered while you are on vacation.

One method is to set the pots in a box filled with peat moss, sawdust, or even soil and soak the filling thoroughly just before you leave. For that matter, pots

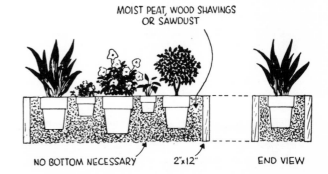

MOIST PEAT, WOOD SHAVINGS OR SAWDUST

NO BOTTOM NECESSARY   2"x12"   END VIEW

imbedded up to their rims in the garden will retain water longer than those left in the open, exposed to sun and drying air. Small pots may also be set inside larger ones in a packing of wet peat moss. Or you can place potted plants on brick, or inverted pots or pot saucers in a laundry tub; or place a soaker so that, when the water is

turned on, plants in containers will be thoroughly covered by the spray.

FERTILIZING AND FEEDING

Because containers hold a relatively small volume of soil, and because nutrients are leached through more readily, plants grown in them should be fed every 2 or 3 months during the active growing season

The average plant in a tub or box, or in a container 18 or more inches square, usually requires feeding only three times a year. The amount of soil in a container of this size serves to retain many of the nutrients provided in fertilizer applications over a comparatively long period. Some fruiting plants, such as citrus, and some shrubs producing heavy crops of flowers, such as camellias, often benefit from an extra feeding.

Always follow the directions that come with the fertilizer just as carefully as you would follow your doctor's prescription.

WEATHER PROTECTION

Container plants expose a large surface area for air to circulate around and are therefore more sensitive to extremes of weather than plants rooted in the soil. This disadvantage is cancelled by their portability for they can easily be moved to escape seasonal extremes.

In hot dry weather, or days with warm winds, keep pots watered, shift them into a sheltered spot. Potted plants located in a hot corner, where they receive the sun's rays directly and by reflection from paving and walls, will need plently of water during summer. In the hot interior valleys, potted plants will not survive a summer unless sheltered from heat.

In cold weather, container plants are more likely to freeze than their relatives in the garden beds. They should be moved to a protected area or covered with some plastic film, burlap, or other lightweight material. If a cold spell catches you unprepared and if your potted or movable plants freeze, take them in immediately before the sun has a chance to thaw them and place them in your garage or in a shaded coldframe or lighted cellar where the air, although above freezing, is cold. Allow them to thaw out as slowly as possible. Annuals which have become badly frozen can seldom be brought back to health, and therefore should be thrown away.

Collapsible pot-and-flat racks can be arranged to protect as well as display. Most protection would be provided by a backing of plastic screen, but a cloth covering will immeasurably aid growing conditions

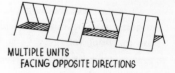

MULTIPLE UNITS
FACING OPPOSITE DIRECTIONS

HOW TO SET A SHRUB IN A TUB

1. *Shrub ready to be transplanted into tub. Can sits on piece of heavy paper that will make the clean-up job easier. Can cutters used to split can down each side.*

2. *After cutting each side, lay can on its side; cut bead at the bottom on both sides so that the can will open easily. Be careful not to damage the foliage.*

3. *Remove loose soil around roots. One or 2 inches of coarse rock added to bottom of container will aid drainage. Add prepared soil mix before setting in.*

4. *Once plant is in the container, fill with soil to 1½ inches from top. This particular mix was made of 1 part soil, 1 part peat, 1 part sand, 2 parts leaf mold.*

5. *When you have finished, water to wet new soil, settle plant in container. Add an inch or two of mulch to help keep surface roots cool and to retain moisture in soil.*

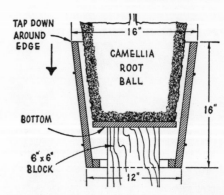

LEFT. *Here is a cleverly designed tub (detail above) that simplifies the technique of root pruning. Design makes inspection of the plant's root system easy. The soil is light, so the tub is easy to lift onto 6x6-inch block. Light tap drops sides to expose roots for pruning.*

ABOVE. *If the plant is rootbound, wait until growth hardens, then remove 1 inch of root mass on one side. Replace plant; fill gap with sand, peat, leaf mold, mix.*

Care of hanging baskets

Before you get involved with hanging baskets, remember that they take even more time and care than ordinary containers. Exposed on all sides to drying air and winds, they dry out faster. Daily watering in hot weather is a must; some plants such as fuchsias and tuberous begonias may need it twice a day. About once every week or 10 days during the hottest weather, take down hanging baskets and soak them in a tub of water until thoroughly saturated. Drain well, then rehang.

To get the lush growth necessary for plants on display, feed them three or four times during the active growing season.

And again, because they are so much in evidence, hanging basket plants need regular grooming—such as pinching and removal of old flowers.

SETTING SHRUBS AND TREES IN TUBS

Some skillful gardeners raise their tubbed plants from seed, seedlings, or cuttings, carefully bringing them along through a succession of pots until they reach tub size. Most gardeners, however, buy their plants from a nursery, either in cans or balled in burlap.

The technique for transplanting from a can to a tub or for setting a balled shrub in a box is basically the same as for planting it in the ground. Here is a rundown on these simple planting techniques:

Transplanting from cans

To make sure that the earth ball will not break up when the can is broken away from it, water the plant thoroughly a few days before planting.

Slit down the side of the can and spread it open. Lift out the plant by placing one hand on top of the root ball and the other underneath.

Gently set the plant in the tub on a soft cushion of loam over a layer of pebbles put in the bottom of the tub for drainage. If properly positioned, the top of the root ball should be about 2 inches below the rim of the tub to provide room for water. Fill in the space between the root ball and the sides of the tub with soil and settle it with water.

Planting balled plants

Setting a balled and burlapped shrub or tree into a tub is simple—the key requirement is gentle handling.

Before planting, soak the root ball in water until bubbles stop rising. Lower the burlapped ball into the tub, setting it gently on a soft bed of loam. Never use the trunk as a handle.

If the top of the ball comes to the right height in the tub, about 2 inches below the rim, pack soil into the space between the burlapped ball and sides until the tub is about three-quarters full. Soak with water, allow the soil to settle, then fill in the remainder. Just before covering over the top of the root ball, cut the twine that secures the burlap around the trunk. The burlap will rot away in time. Soak with a generous watering.

HOW TO MOVE HEAVY CONTAINERS

The first time you bend down to move a good sized container plant, you make two quick discoveries: The container is usually hard to get hold of, and it is heavier than you thought.

A 12-inch clay pot of freshly watered petunias, for instance, tips the scales at about 65 pounds. A rhododendron in a redwood tub 18 inches square and 18 inches high weighs up to 200 pounds. A tree in a box 2 feet square and 2 feet tall may weigh as much as 800 pounds.

If you approach these figures with common sense, you may be looking for some mechanical aids when you start moving flats, pots, tubs, and plant boxes around the garden.

Skids and runners

When you move containers on a smooth surface like concrete or blacktop, often all you need is some way to reduce the friction a little and some kind of "handle" on the container so you can get a good hold on it. Here are three suggestions:

Skid cloth. You have probably seen professional movers put a piece of heavy furniture on a strip of burlap and skid it across a smooth floor. You can use the same technique to move a plant container across a hard surface. Tip the container and work an old throw rug or burlap bag under it. Get a good hand hold, and you'll be surprised at the load you can pull.

A shovel with a wide blade can be used the same way as a skid cloth for moving across the ground, a rough surface like exposed aggregate, or even a lawn (but not brick or any other surface the shovel might scratch). A wide-blade shovel with a D handle works well. You can buy a coal shovel with a 13 by 14-inch blade for about $4.

Sled runners. You can make a simple sled with two hardwood runners and a pull rope. Or you might prefer to attach the runners permanently to the container and loop a pull rope around it for moving. The runners lift a plant box off the ground and give it good drainage.

Burlap bag used as a skid cloth to move tub across uneven surface. The bag will wear through quickly on a rough surface so keep some old ones on hand to use.

A flat-bladed shovel can also be used to slide a heavy tub across uneven surfaces. Standard square-pointed shovels accommodate a container with 10-inch base.

Here's how rollers are used to move a large heavy container over a lawn. Note cleats under tub. Use of the three rollers is the traditional Japanese technique.

Rollers

One of the oldest ways to move a heavy, flat bottomed object is on three or four unattached rollers, such as lengths of two-inch pipe. As the container is moved along, you take a roller from behind and put it in front. It is easier to work with four rollers than three. To move a heavy box across a lawn without scarring it, roll it across on a plank. The rollers are not easy to use on rough ground or on a slope.

Turning with rollers; keep close together.

Wheels

Where the surface is firm, the easiest way to move a heavy load is on wheels. Here are some ways to put wheels to work for you in the garden.

Hand truck. A two-wheeled hand truck of the type that movers and warehousemen use is a handy piece of equipment to have around the place if you move many heavy objects. However, except on the very heaviest and most expensive hand trucks, the lifting blade is too short to get under a plant box. To get around this difficulty, use a rope or strap to hold it on the hand truck, or extend the platform with a piece of plywood lashed to the bottom frame. Hand trucks may be rented from most equipment rental firms.

A lawnmower for a hand truck. If you have a lawnmower with a handle that goes past center without lifting

the rollers off the ground, you can easily adapt it to use as a hand truck. Details are shown in the sketch below.

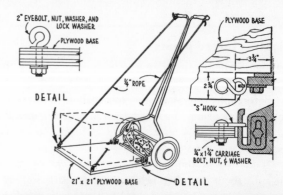

A platform dolly. This little "flat car" that movers use for pianos is good for moving heavy boxes over a smooth surface. It may take two or three men to lift the box a few inches off the ground so the dolly may be slid under, but once the load is balanced, it is easy to move across a good surface.

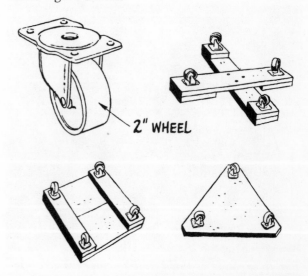

You can make your own dollies with heavy-duty, 2-inch industrial casters mounted on 1-inch plywood or cleats.

You can buy a 500-pound capacity, 4-wheel dolly from a moving supply company. Check with your local hardware stores, too; they may be able to order one for you. They can also be rented.

You can make a dolly with heavy-duty casters mounted on a heavy piece of plywood. A triangular dolly works fine, and 3 wheels cost less than 4. Buy three medium weight, 3-inch industrial casters with composition treads.

Attach casters to the tub. You can, of course, make your tubbed plants permanently mobile by attaching casters to them. However, this has some disadvantages.

If you have a large number of tubbed plants to be mobilized, you may find the cost disproportionate to the convenience. Each tub would require three or four industrial-type swivel casters of good quality and these are not inexpensive. Furthermore, even the best casters are liable to succumb to rust after a few seasons. Water lying on the surface of the patio or seeping from the tub will expose them to rapid corrosion.

If you have only one or two tubbed plants, however, this method may appeal to you. Buy a set of good quality casters with hard-surfaced wheels, either steel or plastic, that are large enough to roll over minor obstructions without hesitation. Ideal minimum would be 2 inches in diameter. Obtain the type with a flat base plate which is pierced with four screw holes.

Before attaching them to the tub bottom, work cup grease thoroughly into the bearing race where the caster swivels. This is the caster's most vulnerable spot. Fasten them to the tub with galvanized bolts.

An alternate method that is less expensive although not quite so convenient is to use fixed wheels instead of the swiveling type. These can be installed in two's instead of three's and four's. They cost less than swiveled types and they are likely to outlast them because they do not have the vulnerable ball bearings.

To use this method, simply fasten a pair on one side of the tub and attach a wooden cleat to the other. To move the tub, you lift the side resting on the cleat and roll the tub on the two wheels like a cart. This plan has one obvious disadvantage: A heavy tub would be hard to lift, because almost half the full weight would have to be hefted before the tub could be tipped far enough for it to be rolled.

A wheelbarrow. You can handle a good sized plant container in a wheelbarrow. The trick is getting the container in and out without strain. Sketch shows how.

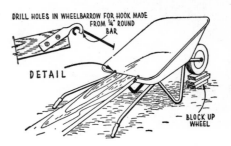

Pull plant boxes in and out on skid cloth.

A coaster wagon. It's useful for carrying a few 12-inch clay pots or a small plant tub or box. The large wheels go over rough surfaces easily. Two people—one pushing and one pulling—can take a heavy load up a steep grade in a well-balanced wagon.

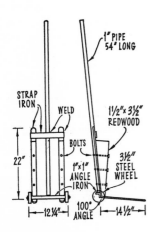

With this home-made hand truck a man can move a tubbed plant weighing 500 pounds or more over a *fairly level surface. Cleats on bottom of tub hold it high enough so metal strips can be slipped underneath.*

White pelargoniums and blue trailing lobelia, lightly shaded by an overhanging branch of Australian tea tree, make a lush display in this 4-foot-square box at the Los Angeles Arboretum.

ANNUALS–PERENNIALS: FOR PORTABLE OUTDOOR COLOR THROUGHOUT THE SEASONS

ANNUALS

Annuals have many qualities that recommend them for container gardening. They bring a rush of color to your garden—no waiting for two years or so for blooms. Their shallow roots adapt readily to pots and boxes.

The secret of success with potted annuals lies in regular care. This means daily watering in warm weather, occasional feeding, and some fussing over—removing faded blossoms, pinching back, staking. A dozen pots will take about 10 minutes daily care. If you can spend the time and have spots which need their sparkling color, annuals definitely are worth the trouble of growing them in containers.

When to plant

Planting season for annuals is the same as for those grown in the ground. However, you have this advantage: in any climate you can advance the calendar by a month or more by sowing seed and bringing along seedlings in protected pots or boxes.

Of course, you can buy annuals in flats at the nursery; most gardeners do.

Soil and fertilizer

Annuals will thrive on the general potting formula or the 50 per cent sand and 50 per cent peat moss U. C. mix recommended in the chapter on container culture. Supply nutrients for rapid growth by feeding with liquid fertilizer after the plants are above ground.

Growing from seed

For the gardener who longs to grow his own flowers from seed but has very little space, raising them in pots offers a happy solution. Not only do you have the fun of growing them, but when they are in bloom, you have a gay and effective display of color for the porch or terrace, or for a vacant spot in the garden.

The annuals you see in the photographs were grown in 8-inch clay "pans" (1 inch lower than regular pots) on an 8 by 12-foot sun deck. In this collection of 24 pots are 2 kinds of dwarf ageratum, some dwarf sweet alyssum, annual candytuft, clarkia, linaria, dwarf marigolds, dwarf double nasturtiums, dwarf phlox, Virginian stock, and dwarf pompon zinnias.

All these annuals are easy to grow, flower from seed in 7 to 18 weeks, and produce masses of color over a long period. They have a dwarf habit (3 to 12 inches) and require no staking to keep them upright. You can sow seeds of these annuals in a standard soil mixture in the open ground after frosts are over. Fill pots with soil mixture to 1¾ inches from the top. Firm and level the mixture with the bottom of a glass jar. Then add 1 inch of screened, sterilized leaf mold and level it with the jar.

Water the pots from the bottom by placing them in a pan or other container that is 9 inches deep. Fill the container with water until it reaches the top of the pots. When the surface of the soil is wet, remove the pots and allow them to drain. On 8-inch labels, write the name of each flower and date of sowing. Insert the label, sow the seed, and cover with damp sterilized leaf mold, pressing lightly. (The smaller the seed, the lighter the covering.)

Place pots rim to rim and cover with several thicknesses of newspaper folded lengthwise; they will cover several pots at a time.

Three days after sowing, start looking for signs of germination. Remove the newspaper as the seedlings start sprouting. Never allow sun to shine on uncovered seedlings. Keep each pot shaded from sun until all seeds have germinated. After seedlings are up, cover the pots with a long piece of cheesecloth, anchoring it on the labels; tuck under the pots, too, if weather is windy. Remove the cheesecloth when the seedlings cover the

RIGHT. *Linaria, nasturtium, candytuft (left to right) in pots set in 8-inch circles in bench. Pots can't tip. Plants are easy to water and saucers below catch the drippings.*

Six weeks after seed was sown (see text), pot-grown annuals looked like this. Benches of 1 by 4-inch boards set on small tables in a protected corner of sun deck.

Potted annuals make a gay display on window ledge. Miniature pompon zinnias and blue and pink dwarf ageratum.

Banked tiers display a pot collection of annuals, perennials at the entrance of this home. The glass shelter stops prevailing wind, protects the pot rack.

Geraniums and petunias are summer standbys in any pot collection. Here they decorate terrace next to entrance drive. Evergreen clematis along eave, on post.

soil completely, and thin out the little plants. If you live in a climate where the sun is very hot, high, light shade is beneficial during the warmest part of the day.

Start overhead watering when seedlings start to develop their second pair of leaves. Use a very fine sprinkler with a light force of water. You can increase the pressure when seedlings are sturdy. In warmer areas, water daily when roots become crowded. When you water, fill each pot to the rim. It usually isn't necesary to feed the plants, since a good potting mixture usually contains sufficient nutrients to maintain growth.

Eleven weeks after sowing—depending on kind— these annuals should be just showing color, in full bloom, or just passing their peak. Here are blooming time-tables:

Bloomed 7 weeks from seed: Virginian stock, *Alyssum* Royal Carpet, Tiny Gem marigold.

Bloomed 12 weeks from seed *Linaria* Fairy Bouquet, Dwarf Double Gem nasturtium, Splendid Mixed candytuft.

Bloomed 14 weeks from seed: *phlox* Dwarf Beauty, *Clarkia elegans* double mixed, Dwarf French Double marigold.

Bloomed 18 weeks from seed: *Ageratum* Blue Ball, *Ageratum* Fairy Pink, *Zinnia* Pompon Pastel mixture.

A dozen reliable annuals

Although you can grow almost all annuals in containers, the following 12 are tried-and-true:

Floss flower *(Ageratum houstonianum).* Blue Perfection most useful, soft lavender-blue flowers combine easily with other colors. Blooms all summer and up until frost. Sun or part shade. 1 to 1¼ feet.

Amethyst flower *(Browallia speciosa).* One of the better plants for container culture. Profuse small violet-blue, white-throated flowers, glossy green foliage. Blooms spring through summer. Tender to frosts. Can be brought into house for winter. Part shade. 1¼ feet.

Balsam *(Impatiens balsamina).* Double or semi-double flowers like miniature roses or camellias in pink, rose, lavender, and white. Compact plants ideally suited for containers. Summer bloom. Shade inland, sun near coast. 1½ to 2 feet.

Lobelia *(L. erinus).* Small soft to deep blue flowers on compact upright or trailing plants. Both types superb for ground covers at base of plants in containers, in hanging pots or baskets. Summer and fall. Shade in hot climates, sun near coast. 4 to 8 inches.

Sweet Alyssum *(Lobularia maritima)*. Invaluable ground cover or carpet with white, lavender, or purple flowers. Comes quickly from seed, re-seeds readily. Blooms most of the year except in cold-winter climates. Sun or part shade. 4 to 8 inches.

Petunia *(P. hybrida)*. Unsurpassed for wide color range, sustained bloom (through winter in mild climates), and easy culture. Dwarf compact types, 9 inches; balcony (trailing) types, 12 inches; large ruffled types, 12 to 15 inches, somewhat more difficult to grow. Sun near coast, part shade in hot inland.

Fairy Primrose *(Primula malacoides)*. Dainty lavender, pink, rose, or white flowers in tiers. If planted early enough in fall, blooms December to May in mild climates. Tender in cold-winter areas. Partial shade. 12 inches.

Primrose *(Primula obconica)*. Perennial, treated as annual. Large flowers in lavender, blue, pink, rose, and white. Hairy leaves may cause some persons to suffer skin irritation. Partial shade. 10 inches.

Poor Man's Orchid, Butterfly Flower *(Schizanthus pinnatus)*. Abundant small orchid-like flowers in soft pink, rose, lilac, purple, and white. Fern-like foliage. Partial shade. Best in cooler coastal areas. 1½ feet.

Cineraria *(Senecio cruentus)*. One of the finest plants for depth and vividness of color—blue, purple, red, crimson, salmon, and white. Free-blooming in shade. Best in cool moist fog belt. Tender to frost. Spring and early summer bloom. 1 to 2 feet.

Marigold *(Tagetes)*. Gay summer annuals makes a surprisingly thrifty container plant. Dwarf varieties most successful. Tall varieties get rangy, need staking, require more space. Smallest is signet marigold *(T. tenuifolia pumila)*—tiny golden orange single flowers on compact plant 8 inches high. Foliage dainty, fern-like. Single and double French marigolds, ½ to 2 feet, in yellow, orange, red, bronze, and combinations of these colors. Sun near coast, part shade inland.

Viola, Tufted Pansy *(Viola cornuta)*. Rewarding container plant available in blue, yellow, apricot, ruby red,

Fern, primroses bring feeling of woodland in spring to terrace. After bloom, set out primroses in garden, replace in box with fibrous or tuberous begonias, lobelia.

Geraniums in two shades of pink—Princess Fiat, soft shrimp; and Fiat Queen, salmon-coral—give summer color at Sunset. Replaced in winter with camellias.

Corsican hellebore blooms several months in late winter, spring. Feed monthly in spring, summer with fertilizer. Cut old stems to base after bloom. Half shade.

Plantain lily (Hosta), *has lush character of plants accustomed to growing near water or in cool shade. These plants in 10-inch pots stand at head of a pool.*

and white. Blue and yellow most floriferous. Combines beautifully with other flowers, especially bulbs. Blooms winter to early summer in mild climates. Partial shade. 8 inches.

PERENNIALS

Many nurseries grow perennials in cans or pots, and by keeping an eye out for those that look particularly trim and thrifty, you can usually choose good container subjects. Although almost everyone enjoys profuse and long bloom in perennials, foliage that remains handsome over a good part of the year is almost as important.

Performance of perennials varies with climate. Many species enjoy cold-winter dormancy, and languish where winters are warm. Practically all perennials take two years to reach maximum size and bloom and at maturity many may require the same size container as a small shrub.

A dozen reliable container subjects

Here are a dozen perennials that give maximum returns —in flowers, foliage, or both—for several months of the year:

Bear's breech *(Acanthus mollis).* Imposing plant with large, lobed, shining, dark green leaves. Spikes of whitish, lilac, or rose flowers with green or purplish bracts. Blooms in late summer. Needs shade inland. Provide large containers. Needs winter protection in cold-winter climates. 3 feet.

Goat's beard *(Astilbe arendsii).* Tiny pink, red, or white flowers in full graceful plumes; divided, fern-like leaves—green on most varieties, rich red on one variety. Best in cool coastal areas. Blooms in summer, leaves die to ground in winter. 1 to 1½ feet.

Begonia. Several kinds make superb container plants. All tender in cold-winter climates.

Fibrous begonia *(B. semperflorens).* Covers itself with bloom in pink, rose, red, or white blooms in summer and fall. Filtered shade; sun near coast. 6 to 18 inches.

Tuberous begonia. Spectacular semi-double or double flowers in yellow, orange, apricot, pink, rose, red, and white. Plants need staking to support heavy flowers. 1 to 2 feet. **Basket begonia** *(B. lloydii).* Tuberous. Cascading stems with prolific single or semi-double blooms in same color range as upright tuberous begonia. Magnificent in hanging containers. Filtered shade.

Pots of chrysanthemums add bright spots of color in Sunset's patio in fall. Cuttings set in spring, grown on in larger pots until buds form, then moved to patio.

Chrysanthemum Smith's Innocence grown as standard. To grow: support cutting with 1-by-1 stake, pinch off at 18 inches, let 6 laterals form head, rub off shoots.

Bellflower *(Campanula isophylla).* Lavender-blue star-shaped blooms in profusion on green-leafed trailing stems. *C. i. alba,* white flowered, considered even more beautiful. *C. i. mayii,* gray-green hairy leaves, has larger blue flowers. All splendid hanging plants. Summer to fall bloom. Part shade.

Florist's Chrysanthemum *(Chrysanthemum morifolium).* Color mainstay for the fall container garden. Wide variety of flower colors and shapes. Can now get varieties that bloom as early as June, others flowering as late as Christmas. Cascade types suitable for hanging containers. Most varieties best in sun. Heights vary from 10 inches to 3 feet.

Elephant's Ear *(Colocasia esculenta).* Huge green arrow-shaped leaves with dark reddish markings. Tender, frosts back in colder mild-winter climates, but comes back in spring from the roots. Excellent for tropical effect. Tubers edible. Sun near coast, partial shade inland. 3 to 5 feet.

Maiden's Wreath *(Francoa ramosa).* Graceful wand-like stems holding sprays of small white or soft pink flowers. Basal clumps of large green, wavy-margined leaves. White form best. Charming in background of

container. Part shade best except along coast. Summer bloom. 2 to 4 feet.

Hellebore *(Helleborus).* Several species, all suitable for containers, but these are outstanding: **Christmas Rose** *(H. niger).* Dark green foliage, white, greenish or purplish-tinged blooms in December to March. 1½ feet. **Lenten Rose** *(H. orientalis),* similar foliage, green to purplish rose flowers February to April. Horticultural forms have flowers variable in color—pink, white, maroon, or purple. 1½ feet. **Corsican hellebore** *(H. lividus,* formerly called *H. corsicus),* most distinctive of all hellebores. Pale blue-green, sharply toothed leaves divided into 3 leaflets. Large clusters of pale chartreuse flowers January to May. To 3 feet. Shade or light shade for all species.

Sea lavender *(Limonium perezii),* formerly called *Statice perezii.* Striking big clusters of tiny purplish lavender flowers flecked white, on slender stems. Basal clumps of large leathery evergreen leaves. Summer to fall bloom. Best in sun in cool coastal areas; can be grown inland in partial shade with ample moisture. Needs winter protection in cold climates. 3 feet.

Lotus *(L. berthelotii).* Trailing 2 to 3-foot stems clothed with fine silvery gray leaves. Scarlet flowers in

Graceful old-timer. Soft green, fluffy asparagus fern (A. sprengeri) sprays over the side of a 17-inch pot.

Exquisite leaf pattern of hardy dwarf dark green fern (Pellea rotundifolia) striking against white gravel.

summer. Sun or part shade. *L. mascaensis.* Upright, to 1 foot, but tends to cascade over edge of containers. Gray leaves; bright yellow sweet pea-shaped flowers in spring. Sun. Both species excellent for hanging pots, need winter protection in cold areas.

Geranium *(Pelargonium).* Lady Washington Pelargonium, Martha Washington Geranium *(P. domesticum).* Dark green, heart-shaped, somewhat crinkly leaves; large showy flowers, azalea-like, in loose rounded clusters. White, and many shades of pink, red, lavender, purple, with brilliant blotchings and markings. 3 feet. **Common Geranium, Garden Geranium** *(P. hortorum).* Probably the most universally popular flowering plant for containers. Round velvety leaves with scalloped margins, often with a broad color zone in center. Single or double flowers in white and many shades of pink, red, and salmon. Sun; filtered shade in hot climates. 3 feet and more. Many other species of pelargonium fine for containers, some with strikingly zoned and colored foliage, others with fragrant leaves also popular for containers. Trailing types such as ivy geranium for hanging containers. All tender outside in cold climates, commonly wintered over indoors or in other protected places.

Showy Sedum *(Sedum spectabile).* Hardy, sturdy succulent with gray blue-green leaves; large flat clusters of small pink, star-shaped flowers in summer, early fall. Sun or part shade. 1½ feet.

Ferns

Ferns are basic container plants in a class all their own. They increase in beauty each time a new frond uncurls and evergreen types retain their luxuriant growth throughout the year. Following are a few of the smaller ferns suitable for containers outside (or indoors under special conditions):

Maidenhair fern *(Adiantum).* **Southern maidenhair** *(A. capillus veneris)* and **California maidenhair** *(A. jordanii)* are native to California, the latter being more widespread. Both make light green fluffy clumps, the stems black and wiry. **Five finger fern,** sometimes called **Western maidenhair** *(A. pedatum)* is also a native from California north to Washington. Wiry black stems support fan-like rays of soft green leaflets.

Mother fern *(Asplenium bulbiferum).* Graceful lacy fronds 2 to 3 feet long arched by weight of plantlets that form on upper side of each frond. Fine in pots, tubs, or directly in ground in protected areas.

Bird's nest fern *(Asplenium nidus).* Nest-like rosette of bright green fronds; 2 to 3 feet high. Pots or tubs. Needs excellent drainage.

Holly fern *(Cyrtomium falcatum).* Thick, glossy, dark green fronds, 1½ to 2 feet long. Dwarf habit of growth. Good for planters and pots. Can also be grown in the open ground. Takes more wind and exposure than most ferns.

Low, white ceramic bowl makes elegant foil for green, arching sprays of asparagus fern on tiled pool edging.

This scooped-out log garden is about 8 by 30 inches, provides natural environment for ferns, succulents.

Western sword fern (*Polystichum munitum*). A clumping type with narrow 3½-foot fronds. Hardy, requiring protection only from scorching sun and drying winds. Good in shade under trees.

New Zealand cliff brake (*Pellaea rotundifolia*). A New Zealand member of the fern family. Fronds, about 1 foot long and 1½ inches across, have brown, hairy stalks; round, dark green leaflets. Likes moist, well

drained soil rich in humus. In mild areas grow outside in filtered shade. Hardy to 30°. In colder areas, move indoors in winter.

Ouvard spider brake (*Pteris serrulata Ouvardii*). Green, ribbon-like fronds to 30 inches long. Fine for contrast with dark camellia foliage. Good in tubs or planters.

Large ferns

Australian tree fern (*Alsophila australis*). Grows to 18 feet. Best of the fast growing tree ferns. Severely damaged by drought; takes months to recover if permitted to dry out. Thrives in almost complete sun along the coast in areas protected from wind.

Tasmanian tree fern (*Dicksonia antarctica*). Slow growing with short, stout trunk. Tree 8 to 10 feet high. Exceptional for exotic and subtropical effect. Dense cluster of large, deep green fronds at the top of the fibrous trunk. Hardiest of all the tree ferns.

Chain fern (*Woodwardia chamissoi*). Soft green fronds 3 to 6 feet, and sometimes to 9 feet long. Will take full sun.

LEFT. *Frilly lace fern* (Polystichum aculeatum) *grows well in garden or pots. Plant eventually gets 3 feet across, but always remains low. New plants form on frond midribs. Insensitive to cold, hardy to 10°-15°.*

North-South covered walk is ideal for growing ferns in wire baskets lined with tree fern trunk, osmunda, sphagnum. Note nozzles for watering above plants.

Hahn's ivy "trees" in Japanese fish tubs flank a white wrought iron stile between terrace and lawn above. Ivy is trained on wires attached to post in center of tub.

CLIMBERS - TRAILERS: TUBBED VINES FOR VERTICAL COLOR; HANGING BASKETS FOR EYE-LEVEL BLOOM

It might surprise some gardeners to learn that almost any vine can be grown successfully in a container—at least for a while, providing it is given careful attention. Under some circumstances, a tubbed vine is the only answer to a planting problem. Where the paved surface of a patio, driveway or loggia fills in to a wall that needs a vine, often the only way of working the vine into the planting scheme is to grow it in a tub parked on the paving. In other instances, an effective screen or traffic barrier can be made with a trellised vine in a movable tub or box. Sturdy trellises can be attached to a tub, and some of them, such as the grids used for espaliering tubbed fruit, provide an attractive background for the vine's tracery. Your only chore aside from watering and feeding is diligent pinching back and training during the active season of growth. Some vines are also well suited for growing as trailers in hanging baskets and window boxes.

Although any vine can be grown in a container for a time, there are a few of them that get along better than the rest. Fast-growing types or those with hawser-like stems outgrow a container rapidly and dwindle. Usually, slow-growing types, such as the ivies; or annual vines that do not put out great root systems; or light, delicate vines will perform best.

Some types that you might hesitate to inflict on your garden because of their greedy and far-wandering roots, can be successfully disciplined in a container.

As a group, vines do not require any special soil considerations. Some of them do have their individual preferences, but most of them will do well in a standard mixture. (See section on potting mixes.)

You do have to keep an eye on root development. Some vines will drive their roots right through the drain holes and into the soil below. If this starts to happen, shift the vine to a larger container.

WHAT TO PLANT

Following is a run-down on vines that may be successfully grown in containers:

Asparagus. Here are the ornamental relatives of the edible asparagus. Some are rampant climbers with runners about 40 feet long, some delicate trailing species, some medium-sized upright shrubs, some dwarfs. Here are the best shrubby or vining types for growing in containers. (All are hardy outdoors to 25°, if moved to a protected spot in winter):

Asparagus fern (*A. plumosus*). Woody climbing vine, which may reach 20 feet or more. Fern-like fronds made up of bright green, 1/4-inch needle-like leaves. Purplish black berries in fall. Variety *A. p. compactus* and *A. p. nanus* are good dwarf forms suitable for pots.

A. sprengeri, although not a fern, is usually called one. Graceful, twiggy, arching stems, with slender, light green, needle-like leaves; fragrant pinkish flowers in summer, bright red berries in winter. Excellent plant for hanging baskets. Drought resistant. Hardy to 24°.

Clematis. Hardy. Some of the more refined deciduous clematis are excellent in containers. When you grow them in tubs, you can enjoy the large, showy flowers up

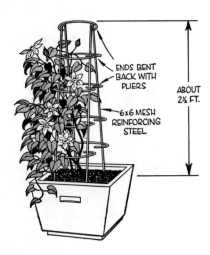

ENDS BENT BACK WITH PLIERS

ABOUT 2½ FT.

6x6 MESH REINFORCING STEEL

close, on the patio. The vine quickly twines itself about the frame, forming a dense mass of foliage. The flowers are always carried on the outside. In fall cut back almost to soil level, and place the tub out of sight, until growth starts again in early spring.

C. jackmanii is strong growing to 20 feet, but easily controlled at 6 feet. Leaves are divided into leaflets. Flowers from July to frost—7-inch wide, purple bloom. Some of the hybrids include: Gypsy Queen, deep violet with wine-crimson in it; Star of India, purple barred with red; Mme. Andre, deep rich crimson; Ramona, sky-

blue flowers. *C. lanuginosa henryi* (often sold as *C. henryi*) is a modest grower excellent for tracery on light frame, trellis, baffle. Very large white flowers, 7 to 9 inches across, in July and August. *Culture:* Since flowers borne on new wood, can be pruned severely in spring. Usually cut back to within 2 joints of the base of last season's new wood. Plant deeply—peg down stem to first joint so it is buried; roots will form along the stem. Stake at time of planting to protect brittle stems.

Cup-and-saucer vine (*Cobaea scandens*). Perennial treated as an annual. Fast growth in warm weather to 20 to 30 feet. Climbs by twining branched tendrils, which cling to rough surfaces without support. Leaves divided into 2 or 3 pairs of oval, 4-inch leaflets. Flowers bell-shaped, first greenish, then violet or rosy purple; also a white-flowered form. *Culture:* Start seeds in 4-inch pot. Notch side of seed with knife before planting. Press edgewise into moist soil. Barely cover seed; keep moist but not wet. Grow in warm sunny location.

Carolina jessamine (*Gelsemium sempervirens*). Evergreen. Hardy to 20°. Moderate growth to 20 feet. Pairs of glistening warm-green 4-inch leaves hang in neat foliage patterns on long streamers. Fragrant tubular, yellow flowers to 1 to 1½ inches long in early spring. *Culture:* No special care. Best in full sun.

Lilac vine (*Hardenbergia comptoniana*). Twining evergreen. Hardy to 20°. Slow growing to 7 to 8 feet. Leaves divided into 3, sometimes 5 dark green oval, or narrower, 2 to 3-inch leaflets. Open growing with foliage casting its shadow in patterns. Masses of deep blue-violet flowers in late winter, early spring; like miniature wistarias at close range, like froth at distance. *Culture:* Grows in sun or shade, best on north or east wall. Prune to help it show its open-pattern qualities.

Ivy (*Hedera*). Two species used freely: Algerian and English ivy. Both climb by aerial rootlets.

Algerian ivy (*H. canariensis*) is only hardy to 20°. More tolerant of hot sun than English ivy. Leaves 5 to 8 inches wide, 3 to 5 lobed, and more widely spaced along the stems than English ivy. Variegated form has leaves edged with greenish white.

English ivy (*H. helix*). Hardy. Leaves dark green with pale veins. On sterile shoots leaves broadly ovate to triangular, 3 to 5 lobed, 2 to 4 inches wide at base and as long. On fertile shoots leaves not lobed and more ovate.

Many small and miniature leafed sports in a variety of foliage forms. *H. h. hahnii*, light green leaves, dense-branching growth. *H. h. conglomerata*, slow-growing dwarf. White and yellow variegated forms interesting against dark backgrounds, many delicately cut forms fine for traceries against brick or stucco. *Culture:* Shade or sun in all but the hot interiors. Small leafed forms more susceptible to sunburn. Algerian ivy best in hot summer climates. Annual trimming and cutting back necessary to keep ivy from getting bunchy.

Wax plant *(Hoya carnosa).* Evergreen. Twining plant with small aerial rootlets. Grown as an indoor plant except in warm climates where temperatures don't drop below 30° in winter. Stiff, succulent, wax-like leaves, red when small, turning green as they mature. Very fragrant flowers tightly fit into almost perfect clusters of creamy velvet white. In the center of each flower is a perfect 5-pointed star with a dark pink center. *Culture:* Best in partial shade at temperatures of 70° or more. During growing season, water deeply, let soil partially dry out between soakings. In cool climates allow to go dormant in winter, water only enough to keep leaves from shriveling.

Australian bluebell creeper *(Sollya fusiformis).* Evergreen. Hardy to 25°. Low climber or trailing sub-shrub with pale green, dainty, glossy, 1 to 2-inch leaves on delicate, twining stems. Masses of brilliant blue, ½-inch bell-shaped flowers through most of the summer. Place potted vine on a low wall where branches can spill down over the side. *Culture:* Full sun or part shade in coastal areas, part shade inland. Water generously.

Madagascar jasmine *(Stephanotis floribunda).* Evergreen. Hardy outdoors to 30°. Woody climber to 10 to 15 feet. Glossy green, leathery, 4-inch long leaves. Fragrant white funnel-shaped, 1 to 2-inch flowers carried in loose open clusters. *Culture:* Indoors, rest plants in winter by keeping them on the dry side and at 55°. Grow in partial shade outdoors.

Star jasmine *(Trachelospermum jasminoides).* Evergreen. Hardy to 20°. Twining on slender stems to 20 feet. Leaves sturdy, glossy dark green. Small white very fragrant flowers in loose clusters. *Culture:* Must be supported. Use heavy string or cord to lead stems in right direction. Train where fragrance can be enjoyed and night lighting can pick out the starry blooms. Grow in sun or shade.

Sweet peas. A box or tub of sweet peas is no substitute for a 50-foot row along the back fence, but for many gardeners, it's much more practical. You get lots of color in a small space; you can move the container onto the scene when flowers bloom, and remove it when they fade; and you have the fun of trying something different.

A box 14 inches square makes a good size container for a frame such as the one shown in the top sketch on this page. Drive a 1-inch wooden stake 6 feet long into

the soil in the center of the box. Then, cut up ½-inch square stakes, to make a frame for the top as shown in the sketch. This one measures approximately half the diameter of the box. For the crosspieces of the frame use one 10-inch length and two 4¾-inch lengths. Miter

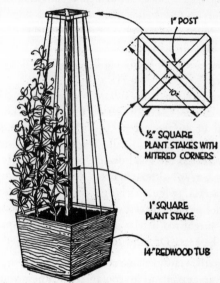

the ends of the four side pieces and toenail them to the diagonals. Nail the square frame to the top of the 1-inch stake. Run strings from the frame to the rim of the tub. Fasten them to the rim with staples.

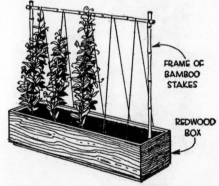

Bamboo poles should make an attractive framework for vines in a long planter such as the one illustrated. Tie them securely together with thongs, since nails are apt to split the poles. When the frame is rigid, run strings from the top of it to the rim of the planter box, holding them taut with staples.

TRAILING PLANTS FOR HANGING BASKETS

Here is a rundown on the plants that do best in hanging baskets (see page 24 for cultural techniques):

Shrimp plant *(Beloperone guttata).* The showy parts of this plant are the spikes of imbricated pinkish or reddish brown bracts which appear in profusion at the ends of 18-inch stems from late spring to fall. A gorgeous sight in full flower in a hanging pot. There now is available a chartreuse flowered form of beloperone.

Amethyst flower (*Browallia*). There are two forms suitable for hanging baskets in lightly shaded spots. *B. americana* is an annual; grows upright in the ground, but will trail in a basket. The small blue or white flowers are carried in profusion. *B. speciosa,* see description in chapter on annuals, page 30.

Bellflower (*Campanula*). *C. fragilis* has gray-green leaves and pale blue star-shaped flowers; *C. isophylla,* large pale blue flowers; *C. isophylla mayi,* gray foliaged form with light blue star-shaped flowers. Give campanulas afternoon shade.

Chrysanthemum. Try the cascade types in sun or very light shade.

Coleus. There is a hanging basket type which, if pinched to encouraged bushiness, makes an attractive trailing foliage plant. But even the usual forms will adapt themselves to this use.

Morning glory (*Convolvulus*). Bush morning glory (*C. cneorum*) has silky gray leaves and white flowers. Plant usually grows to 2 or 3 feet. Blooms from late spring through summer. Requires sun and good drainage. Ground morning glory (*C. mauritanicus*) makes a spreading mat of trailing stems with gray-green leaves. Lots of lavender-blue flowers bloom for months. Prefers partial shade in warm climates, but full sun in cool sections.

Lobelia. This leads any list of trailing plants. The low growing, small flowered annual lobelias are varieties of *L. erinus,* and all are in shades of blue. Sapphire, dark blue blossoms and white eyes, is naturally trailing; however, it is not as floriferous as some of the compact varieties such as Emperor William, which tends to billow over edge of containers. Sun on coast; shade inland.

Fuchsia. Hanging forms are available. However, one bushy, soft-stemmed plant in the center of an 8-inch pot will make a good hanging fuchsia. For quicker effect set 3 small plants in a 10-inch pot. Pinch back branches, never allow fruits to form. Remove flowers as they fade.

Lotus (*L. berthelotii*). This gray foliage perennial has narrow linear leaves on long trailing stems, with scarlet flowers quite typical of the pea family. It must have good drainage and sun. Hardy to about 28°. Pinch back the stems occasionally to keep them from becoming too straggly and spray frequently with a summer oil solution to control mealy bug.

Pelargonium (Martha Washington geraniums, common garden geraniums, ivy geraniums, scented gerani-

ums). Some nurserymen carry a salmon pink flowered variety of Martha Washington geranium (*P. domesticum*) called Santa Cruz that trails naturally over the sides of a container. Princess Victoria, also known as Enchantress, is a variety of ivy geranium (*P. peltatum*) that is popular for hanging pots and baskets. Its large semi-double flowers vary in color according to exposure; in sun they are pink with rose stippling; in shade they are white with pink stippling. The leaves are white edged with rose red. This variety is notorious for reverting; it often sports and sends out a branch with leaves that are all rose-red. Give some shade in hot sections. Peppermint geranium (*P. tomentosum*) is a beautiful trailer with fuzzy silvery green leaves and a sharp, clean, minty fragrance. Grows more lush in filtered light.

Strawberry geranium (*Saxifraga sarmentosa*). Round hairy leaves with prominent light veins. Sends out runners like a strawberry; a new plant forms at the end. White flowers are small and profuse.

Sedum. Two species make especially good container plants. Donkey's trail (*S. morganianum*) is a trailing succulent with interesting form. Best in partial shade except near coast. *S. sieboldii* makes an ideal hanging pot plant—forming a symmetrical rosette, with pendant stems 10 to 12 inches long. Covered with fluffy pink flowers in late summer and early fall. Leaves are gray-green, turn ruddy in autumn. Beautiful under lath where it gets filtered light; needs more sun along coast.

Poor man's orchid (*Schizanthus*). Surprisingly effective in hanging baskets. Late spring and early summer bloom. Early in growth, pinch plants to make them compact, then let them trail. Pansy faced flowers in mostly pastel colors. Light ferny foliage. Filtered shade.

Clock vine, black-eyed Susan vine (*Thunbergia alata*). Annual trailer with orange, apricot, buff, white flowers with black centers. Requires sun to give good bloom, but appreciates shade from hot afternoon sun. Usually grown from seeds, because plants are not easily obtained. Since the seeds have hard coats and germinate slowly, it may take two weeks or more for growth to start.

Wishbone flower (*Torenia fournieri*). An annual which can be sown in spring for hanging containers. Should be sown in flats. Bears a profusion of light blue tubular flowers in summer and fall. Part shade.

Nasturtium (*Tropaeolum majus*). Rapid growing trailing perennial grown as an annual. Can be sown in spring for hanging containers. Bright green round leaves; a profusion of fragrant large flowers in reds and yellows, striped and spotted with darker red or brown. Full sun or light shade.

Snow white hyacinths backed by a large pot of pink and white bleeding heart, and blue and white hyacinths interplanted with white Primula malacoides. *Replaced by yellow tulips, forget-me-nots.*

BULBS: "NATURALS" AS CONTAINER PLANTS— BRIGHT, CLEAN COLOR FOR THE POT GARDEN

Once you recognize the advantages of growing bulbs in pots, you'll want to select a few choice varieties for this purpose each year. Here is what potted bulbs offer you:

1. early spring color indoors or on the terrace,
2. protection of bulbs from gophers,
3. and absence of that untidy after-flower period in the garden.

Most of the spring flowering bulbs grown in containers bloom about 10 days or so ahead of those planted in the open ground. The extra protection of the containers, the faster warming of the soil by the sun, and the crowding of the roots all probably help to account for the difference.

The principle of growing bulbs in pots is essentially the same as growing them in the ground. Drainage should be good and bulbs should be kept moist but not wet during the growing period. Select firm, top-size bulbs. If you want flowers by Christmas, choose early flowering species such as Chinese sacred lilies, paper white narcissus, or early single or double tulips.

SOIL MIXTURE

A good soil mixture for bulbs in pots consists of 2 or 3 parts garden loam (amount depends on whether loam is heavy or medium in texture), 1 part sand, and 1 part leaf mold. One quarter part bonemeal may be worked into this standard potting mixture. Or before planting the bulbs, you may scatter a small handful (this is sufficient for a 7-inch pot) over the surface of the first inch of soil in the bottom of the pot.

The number of bulbs you plant in a pot is generally determined by the size of the bulbs and pot. You can put about 3 large bulbs in a 7-inch pot. Or for a solid mass of color, plant bulbs closer together—almost touching each other. You can put as many as 6 jumbo, double-nosed daffodils in an 8-inch pot; 10 or 11 tulip bulbs. After placing broken crock or pebbles in the bottom, fill the pot about ⅓ full of soil and set the bulbs on top.

Fill in around the bulbs until the tips are barely covered. Leave an inch of space between the soil surface and the rim of the pot for watering. If you are planting several kinds, be sure to label them

Forcing potted bulbs

After the bulbs are planted, water the pots thoroughly. Next place the pots in a cool, dark, or shaded place and keep them there until the bulbs have formed roots. Usual procedure for forced bulbs is to bury the pots in a trench or coldframe and cover them with 6 inches of peat, leaf mold, or soil.

After 7 to 10 weeks, lift a few pots and check to see if roots have formed. When roots have put on good growth, they will be visible through the hole in the bottom of the pot and will form a close network around the outside of the soil ball. At this stage, leaves of some bulbs may be several inches high, but will be pale yellow or white from lack of light.

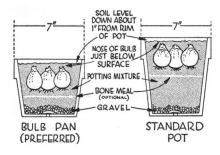

After the bulbs are uncovered and exposed to light, the foliage will start turning green. To force the bulbs to bloom early, move them into warmth indoors or into a greenhouse. From this point and until after flowering, water regularly. Make two or three applications of balanced liquid fertilizer during active growth—between the time the leaves form and the buds show color.

After bulbs have finished flowering, move them off-stage, but don't cut off the foliage. Keep them watered until the foliage begins to yellow. Then gradually withhold water until the pots are completely dried out. When both foliage and soil are dry, knock the soil from the bulbs and plant them in the garden or store them in labeled boxes or paper or string mesh bags for fall planting. (Bulbs cannot be satisfactorily forced two years in succession.)

RIGHT. *3. Space bulbs in pot so they are not crowded around the edge nor bunched too closely in center.*

JOHN ROBINSON

To POT BULBS. *1. Take a clean shallow terra-cotta bulb pan, and cover bottom with broken crock or pebbles.*

2. If bonemeal was not mixed into a standard potting mix, add it now—in lower inch of soil in bulb pan.

Yellow Mammoth crocus, planted in pots, boxes in fall, brought this rich reward to a terrace the next February.

Fragrant hyacinths in pots around mugho pine in redwood box. For prime size, plant new hyacinths yearly.

Growing bulbs without forcing

If you aren't concerned about getting very early bloom, try growing bulbs in pots without forcing them—that is, burying them—as discussed above.

Use the same potting mixture and method as for bulbs to be forced. But instead of burying the pots, simply plunge them to the rim in boxes, frames, or beds of peat moss or sawdust in a cool shaded place. Instead of a 6-inch mulch on top, cover with burlap sacks or inverted flats. Or, you can get by without covering at all if pots are kept moist. The important thing is to keep the bulbs cool until roots have formed.

What to plant?

Here is a selection of the best performers in containers:

Achimenes. Tender tuber closely related to gloxinia and treated in the same way. 1 to 2 feet tall. Flowers borne in axils of the leaves, tubular, 1 to 3 inches across, pink, blue, orchid, lavender, and purple. Bloom in summer. *Culture:* Plant any time after January 15 in acid soil; equal parts of sandy loam and leaf mold make a good mix for pot culture. Also in hanging baskets. Keep soil moist. Grow in partial shade. When plants die back in fall dig and store tubers same as tuberous begonias.

Begonias, tuberous. Tuber. 10 to 18 inches tall. Many varieties with blooms 5 to 8 inches across: camellia flowered type, which resembles its namesake; carnation flowered or fimbriata; crispa, or single frilled type; ruffled double, a cross between the carnation or fimbriata and

camellia forms; and the rose form, with long smooth petals. Colors: in shades of pink, red, yellow, apricot, and white; also Picotee, a camellia flowered form with contrasting color along edges of petals. Bloom July through September. *Culture:* Start tubers in coarse hardwood leaf mold or other similar coarse material when buds begin to swell—late January or early February. Keep moist, but not wet. When growth about 3 inches high transplant tubers to pots or wooden boxes—1 to a 6 or 8-inch container. Plant so tuber just below the soil surface, leaves pointing out. Use a soil mix rich in leaf mold, well-drained. Grow plants in partial shade. Keep soil moist. Dig and store when plants begin to die back in fall.

Kafir lily *(Clivia).* Bulb-like. Tender. 18 inches tall. Dark green, lustrous, strap-shaped leaves. Flowers on stiff stems in rounded clusters vary in color—orange and red tones. *Culture:* Grow in relatively small pot. Repot only once every 3 or 4 years in spring or fall. Prefer rich, fairly heavy soil. Keep moist, but not wet, in full shade. Fertilize with liquid; feed occasionally. When growth slow in fall, reduce watering. Can be grown indoors in cold winter areas.

Autumn crocus *(Colchicum).* Corm. Hardy. Broad basal leaves 4 to 12 inches high in spring, yellowing in June. Showy, cup-like, lavender, rosy-lilac, or white flowers that resemble a true crocus. Blooms from August to September on bare stems. *Culture:* Best in partial shade, in damp, loamy soil. Plant as soon as dormant or immediately after flowering.

Rich pink Mariette lily-like tulips repeat color of one-inch heads of alpine thrift in the terra-cotta bowl.

Daffodils sparkle around tree on a terrace. The giant, Diotima in 8 by 32-inch, Twink in 16 by 16-inch boxes.

Crocus. Corm. Hardy. Clean, deep green, grass-like basal foliage which disappears after the flowers fade. Showy, long-tubed, cup-shaped flowers in shades of yellow, orange, lavender, purple, or white. For kinds that will bloom from September to February, select species according to bloom period. *Culture:* Like sun, but will tolerate light shade. Withhold water in summer. Can grow undisturbed in same pot for several seasons.

Florist cyclamen *(C. indicum).* Probably the best for pot culture. Tuber. Tender to half hardy. Rounded leaves green or sometimes variegated. Many forms available in white and shades of pink or rose. Large flowers on 6 to 8-inch stems appear high above the foliage from November to April. *Culture:* Similar to tuberous begonias. Best in filtered shade. A slightly acid, rich porous soil containing plenty of leaf mold is ideal. Plant tubers in September with the upper portion above the soil level. Keep slightly on the dry side during their dormant period —late June to August or September. Keep moist during the growing season. Grow indoors in a cool room in cold winter areas.

Daffodils. Hardy. Bulb. These are about the easiest of all the bulbs to grow and about the most consistent performers. Choose early, midseason, and late varieties for a long span of color—December or January to April; and remember that King Alfred, the pure yellow trumpet type, isn't the only variety. Height 12 to 16 inches. Other good performers in the Sunset garden: Beersheba,

white trumpet, midseason; John Evelyn, large-cupped, deep yellow cup, white petals, midseason; Unsurpassable, yellow trumpet, early; Diotima, yellow trumpet, early; Texas, double, pale yellow interspread with brilliant orange, early. *Culture:* Plant bulbs in early to late fall. When foliage several inches high, move to full sun, or lightly filtered shade to develop flower buds.

Freesia. Bulb-like corm. Tender, hardy outdoors only where ground does not freeze. Slender, stiff, wiry stems, 12 to 18 inches high; broad grass-like leaves; tubular fragrant flowers in early spring. *F. hybrida,* large flowered form with rose, lavender, mauve, purple, yellow, or orange flowers. Sweetly fragrant. *Culture:* Plant bulbs from August to November and set pots in the sun. Repot when clumps get crowded.

Blood Lily *(Haemanthus katherinae).* Bulb. Tender South African plant. Nearly evergreen, to 3 feet with broad tapering light green leaves, drooping gracefully in umbrella fashion on a short stem. Spectacular bright red flowers in rounded cluster, 9 inches across, open successively over 2 to 4-week period in summer; rise above foliage on leafless stalk. *Culture:* Plant bulbs singly in 8 to 10-inch pot in January or February. Until leaves appear, water only when soil feels dry. Keep in warm room 70° day, 50-55° night for first 8 to 10 weeks. As soon as leaves appear, water thoroughly and keep soil moist. Start feeding once a month with balanced liquid fertilizer. Flower stalks will form in late April or early

Blue Perfection tulips—75 of them of bright violet with white base—bloom in king-sized redwood planter.

Ten rose-pink hyacinths and a dozen or two sky blue grape hyacinths (muscari) *give an entry arrangement.*

May. Grow outdoors in warm, sheltered spot in summer. Give light shade when flowers form so they will last longer. Keep growing vigorously until October then let dry out gradually in cool place. Grow in same pot several years, only replacing some of the top soil each season.

Giant Amaryllis *(Hippeastrum hybridum).* Bulb. Half hardy. Practically evergreen, broad strap-shaped leaves. Sturdy 2-foot stems carry 2 to 4 large lily-like flowers in bright orange, red, or white with stripes and blotches. Also pure white. Bloom: December to June. *Culture:* Pot bulbs in November to December. Set a 3-inch bulb in a 7-inch pot, larger bulbs in correspondingly larger pots. Plant with 1/3 of bulb above the soil surface. Keep slightly moist until growth starts, then increase watering. Keep potted bulbs in cool partially shaded spot, 50° or below. After flowering, plunge pots in garden beds, or knock out of pot and plant direct in garden. Keep growing vigorously as long as possible to build up bulb for next year's flowers.

Hyacinth *(Hyacinthus orientalis).* Bulb. Hardy. Grows 8 to 18 inches high with bright green lance-shaped, fleshy, basal leaves. Fragrant bell-shaped flowers in dense terminal spikes on stout stems in March and April. Single and double flowered forms in white, light and dark pink, shades of blue and purple. *Culture:* Sun loving, but tolerates moderate shade. Plant September and October. If buds appear while stems still short,

put cardboard collar around plant to draw stems up. Bring onto terrace or in house just before buds open.

Lilies *(Lilium).* Bulb. Hardy. 2 to 8 feet high. Bloom summer to fall depending on kind. You can grow with little trouble almost any kind of lilies in containers. Choose varieties with good-looking foliage—and if you don't want to bother with staking—the lower growing ones, such as the white Croft lily, or the rich yellow and red Mid-Century Hybrids. But in larger containers, with proper staking, you can also grow taller kinds such as the white, pink-flushed Olympic Hybrids, the white through yellow into orange Aurelian Hybrids, the Golden Chalice Strain, the white with purple Regal lily, and the pink, carmine-spotted *Lilium speciosum rubrum. Culture:* Plant bulbs in fall. Flowers of all lilies last longer if pots are placed in light shade. Place top-size bulb in 8-inch pot—equal parts loam and rotted leaf mold or peat moss, 1/2 part sand is good. Lilies generally require more humus in soil. Plant base rooting lilies, those that form roots at the base of the bulb, with 1 inch of soil over the top; stem-rooting lilies, those which also root from the stem above the bulb, with 3 inches over top. Place bulb on a cushion of sand, surround with sand before filling in with the soil mix. Water well after planting. Keep in cool shady spot. When 6 inches high, begin to feed monthly with mild liquid fertilizer. Never let the bulbs dry out.

Tuberose *(Polianthes tuberosa).* Tuber. Tender. Sturdy plant with long, narrow, bright green basal leaves.

Regal lilies in large plant tub shine against glossy green background of citrus in Sunset's inner patio.

Golden daffodils—planted in fall in square containers —are displayed handsomely in a large redwood box.

Flower stems 2 to 3½ feet high, bear narrow spikes of heavily fragrant, pure white, funnel-shaped flowers. Blossoms in late spring, intermittently through summer and into fall. *Culture:* Plant in sun. Like plenty of heat and moisture. Can't tolerate alkaline water. Pot any time from January to June. Water sparingly at first, freely after well rooted. After foliage dies down in fall, store pots in warm dry place.

Squill *(Scilla).* Hardy bulb. Plants with narrow basal leaves, white, lilac, blue, pink, or rose flowers in terminal spikes. *S. amoena* to 6 inches, wheel-shaped flowers blue to white in 4 to 6-inch clusters in spring; *S. autumnalis* to 6 inches, rose colored flowers in July to September; *S. hispanica* vigorous 20-inch plant, nodding 1-inch flowers, 12 or more on a spike in May and June, blue and white varieties best; *S. peruviana*, to 1 foot, star-shaped ½-inch flowers in dense clusters in early spring, bluish purple or reddish purple, also a white variety; *S. siberica*, to 6 inches, deep blue nodding ½-inch flowers, 3 or more on spike in early spring. Best in cold winter areas. *Culture:* Grows in sun or shade. Plant bulbs in October or November. Don't have to be transplanted for years. Require lots of moisture.

Gloxinia *(Sinningia speciosa).* Tuber. Tender. Grows to 6 inches tall. Fuzzy velvety, oblong leaves. Large, bell-shaped flowers, heavily ruffled along the edges, in bright clear colors—blues, purples, pinks, reds, and a pure white. Some are blotched or spotted with darker colors. *Culture:* Plant between December and March. Start the same way you start tuberous begonias. Don't get water on foliage, or it spots. Best where humidity high, night temperatures not under 50°. Feed regularly through growing season with fish emulsion or similar mild liquid feed. After flowering gradually withhold water until plants completely dormant. Keep tubers just damp enough to keep them from shriveling until they show active signs of growth. Repot.

Tulip *(Tulipa).* Hardy bulb. Divided into two groups: early flowering and May flowering, and 16 classifications according to shape of flower and growth habit. The Darwins are very large egg- or cup-shaped flowers with a square base on sturdy stems up to 30 inches, in a full range of colors, also with shades of contrasting colors. Good varieties: Blue Perfection, violet with white base, blue ring, large flower, midseason, medium height; Clara Butt, salmon pink, medium-sized flower, late, short. Cottage tulips have rather open flowers with pointed petals on 18 to 30 inch stems. Good varieties: Smiling Queen, dark pink edged with silver, large flower, midseason, tall; Golden Harvest, lemon yellow, early flowering, medium-sized flower, tall; White City, pure white, large flower in midseason, tall grower. *Culture:* Plant in September to October in cold winter areas, but delay until November in warm winter sections. Like full sun except when May temperatures unusually high.

Three tank ends, supported on lava rocks, planted with **Portulacaria afra, Echeveria elegans,** *sedums.*

SUCCULENTS: REWARDING CONTAINER SUBJECTS— AND EASIEST OF ALL TO GROW

Succulents are nearly perfect container plants. They are easy to plant, easy to grow, good looking all year, and they live a long time. Many kinds can be grown indoors or outdoors.

In nature, succulents usually live in a lean, sandy, well drained soil. We can duplicate it by mixing 2 parts coarse sand, 1 part loam, 1 part leaf mold, and $1/2$ part granulated charcoal. Drainage in pots must be perfect.

Succulents do best in small containers. For plants of a rounded form, use a pot 1 inch wider than the diameter of the plant. For tall growing plants, select a pot half as wide as the plant is tall. Unglazed standard clay pots are preferable, but glazed containers are satisfactory if they have a large drainage hole. The potting soil for succulents should be on the dry side. Do not water the newly set plants for several days, then very sparingly for the first month or two. This allows bruised

and broken roots to heal in the dry soil. They're apt to rot if watered heavily.

Before watering check established plants by making a scratch on the soil a half inch deep with a match stick. If the soil appears dry at that depth, water the plant thoroughly from the top of the pot. Soaking the pot in a pan of water or wetting the foliage continually (especially late in the day) may rot succulents.

In summer succulents in containers can get along with water once a week; if the weather is cool and moist, they may need it only once every two or three weeks. When the weather turns cool in fall, rest succulents by watering just enough to keep them from shriveling. This dry rest also hardens the plants against winter cold and rot. Winter rains will more than suffice for container plants exposed outdoors. In March or April, as the plants start making new growth, gradually increase watering.

CLYDE CHILDRESS

Crassula *and* kalanchoe *contribute year-around interest.*

ERNEST BRAUN

Contrasting: sempervivum, echeveria, and crassula.

In a giant metal dish container (tank top). Simple form of the large low round container is a perfect foil for the varied sculptured forms of the succulents.

Succulents in the home should be given all possible sunlight, especially during the winter. A light curtain may be necessary, however, on the brightest summer days to prevent burning of some tender varieties. Winter temperatures should be kept above 40°, although many kinds can be grown outdoors where the temperature is 25° or lower. Good ventilation is desirable.

Here is a basic collection, chosen from 7 major succulent families, which may help to show the range and relationship of these wonderful plants, though it barely opens the door into the succulent world. In all, there are over 20 plant families which include succulents, and the number of individual species, varieties and horticultural hybrids runs into the thousands.

I. Lily family (*Liliaceae*)

Aloe. A very large group of spectacular flowering plants from South Africa. Brilliant "red-hot-poker" blooms rise from a rosette of pointed leaves. The dwarf *A. aristata* is an excellent pot plant.

Gasteria. Two-ranked, straplike leaves, beautifully marked and spotted. Spikes of showy blooms. *G. maculata,* a fine pot plant, thrives in light shade.

Haworthia. Choice small rosette plants with interestingly marked leaves. *H. fasciata,* excellent pot plant. White zebra stripes band the fat pointed leaves.

II. Amaryllis family (*Amaryllidaceae*)

Agave. A highly ornamental group, includes the well-known century plant *(A. americana). A. victoriae-reginae,* an elegant small trunkless plant unlike the other agaves. Compact globe of dark green, each leaf margined white. Blooms yellowish green, 1¼ inches long. Slow growing to 12 inches in diameter. Hardy to 18°.

III. Carpetweed family (*Aizoaceae*)

Faucaria tigrina. Often called tiger jaws. Small rosettes with toothed leaves and large yellow blossoms in fall. *F. tigrina superba,* pale blue-green leaves heavily spotted white. Very good pot plant.

Lithops. Curious small "mimicry plants" that imitate in color and form the pebbles among which they grow. Bright flowers in autumn. Best indoors. *L. bella* a popular species. Lithops must be rested from June to August.

Pleiospilos. These gray-green "split rocks" so closely resemble the native stones among which they grow that

Shallow clay pots with succulents sit on wall along pool. In pots on pool floor are horsetail and papyrus.

Pots of succulents along concrete block wall. Background: New Zealand flax, marguerites, and alyssum.

they are difficult to find except when in flower. The blooms are stemless or short-stalked, solitary or sometimes several, yellow or red. *P. nelii,* a great curiosity, easily grown.

IV. Euphorbia family (Euphorbiaceae)

Euphorbia. A very large group of plants many of which are succulents ranging from the popular crown of thorns, *E. splendens,* to the odd, snake-like medusa's head, *E. caput-medusae.* A characteristic common to most members of the euphorbia family is a thick white milky juice called latex. Flowers usually small, not striking; when ripe, seeds explode, often scattering some distance.

V. Crassula family (Crassulaceae)

Crassula. A very large genus from South Africa, ranging from the flattened gray-green leaves of *C. falcata (Rochea falcata)* with its scarlet blooms in September, the delicate branches of *C. perforata,* to the flattened "silver-dollar" rosettes of *C. hemisphaerica.*

Echeveria. These handsome flowering rosettes from Mexico and South America are superb container plants. The smooth varieties like sun; the hairy leafed forms

like some shade. *E. pulvinata* has soft green plush leaves margined red, blooms with large crimson bells in midwinter. *E. derenbergii* forms tiny, smooth rosettes tipped red. Fine spring bloom. *E. rosea grandis* grows as large as a cabbage, with glossy, waxed leaves tinged red. *E. elegans*—small white rosettes—flowers in spring.

Sempervivum. Often called houseleeks. *S. arachnoideum,* tiny rosettes covered with white cobweb hairs. *S. calcareum,* blue-gray, red-tipped dense rosettes winter hardy in rock gardens anywhere.

Sedum. These are the stonecrops, natural rock plants. *S. dasyphyllum* makes tiny, gray-green tufts, an excellent

Succulents easy to grow from offsets, divisions. Gift collection here in 3, 4-inch pots, in pot of dolomite.

Terra-cotta planter, 18 inches square. The succulents are cobweb sempervivums. Designer is C. Jacques Hahn.

Sand-blasted redwood box of 2-inch stock has mitered corners, beveled edge. Plant is Echeveria pulvinata.

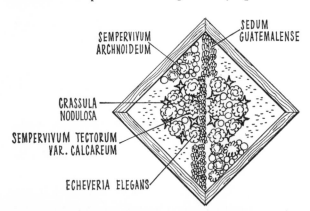

SEDUM GUATEMALENSE

SEMPERVIVUM ARCHNOIDEUM

CRASSULA NODULOSA

SEMPERVIVUM TECTORUM VAR. CALCAREUM

ECHEVERIA ELEGANS

ABOVE. *Plant a mosaic with succulents after first working out a design on paper (see diagram left center). Mulch with sand or white gravel. Water sparingly.*

Shallow box with sun-loving grays: Euphorbia myrsinites, *upper right;* dusty miller (Centaurea candidissima) *on either side;* Aeonium canariense (succulent), *foreground.*

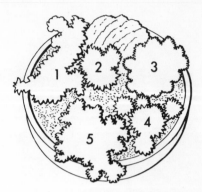

Collection of miniatures: (1) Sedum spathulifolium, *blue-gray foliage; (2)* Androsace primuloides,
*alpine with clusters of lavender-
pink flowers; (3)* Saxifraga decipi-
ens *Apple Blossom, pink flowers
(4)* sempervivum; *(5)* Sedum
spathulifolium *Cape Blanco, smaller form of plant above.*

ground cover. *S. spectabile,* a bright pink, fall flowering
perennial 1 foot high. *S. morganianum,* the silver burro's
tail, a fine hanging basket plant. *S. stahlii,* tiny coral
bead-like leaves; color best in sun. *S. spathulifolium,* a
native of the Oregon coast, has clumps of small rosettes
of roundish leaves covered with bluish white powder;
var. purpureum, leaves tinged with purple-red; Cape
Blanco, horticultural variety grown from a silvery form
of *S. spathulifolium.* All carry bright yellow flowers.

Kalanchoe. Very beautiful flowering succulents,
mostly from Madagascar in Africa. *K. blossfeldiana,*
large clusters of fine red bloom to 12 inches tall; horticultural varieties—Brilliant Star, fiery red, large flowers;
Ernst Thiede, a free-flowering red, dwarf and compact;
Yellow Darling, bright yellow flowers, low growing.

VI. Milkweed family (Asclepiadaceae)

The milkweeds have contributed several odd succulent
forms; these are generally from South Africa.

Stapelia. Often called the carrion flowers, are the
strangest in this family. Small, stiff-angled stems bearing
large and beautiful star-shaped flowers sometimes un-
pleasantly odorous. *S. variegata* and *S. grandiflora* are
two recommended species among the approximately 100
kinds available.

Ceropegias, range from vines to shrubby forms. *C.
woodii,* a popular tuberous trailing vine with variegated
heart-shaped leaves and curious purple balloon flowers.

VII. Composite family (Compositae)

Sometimes called daisy or aster family. This family has
several succulent members, two of which are especially
worth considering as pot plants.

Kleinia repens, a stiff, finger-like plant, striking blue-
green in color. *K. tomentosa's* stiff stems entirely covered
with a snowy felt. *Kleinia scaposa* is an intriguing plant
with long cylindrical, sometimes flattened leaves. *K. sta-
peliaeformis,* fleshy angled stems, small rough leaves
reminiscent of some stapelias.

SEVEN WAYS TO START SUCCULENTS

You can start succulents in at least seven ways: from
seed, stem cuttings, leaf cuttings, whole leaves, divisions,

Jade plant Crassula *covered with pink winter bloom. Older plants have a picturesque character. A house plant in cold areas. A vigorous grower, needs large pot.*

Slow growing succulents are ideal for rock planting, but conifers and small shrubs also do very well. To water plants, let water from hose drip slowly over rock.

offsets (small plants at the base of the parent plant), and proliferations (little sprouts that grow out of leaf margins or along flower stalks). For a lot of succulents in a short time, make cuttings or divisions.

Cuttings

To start stem cuttings in flats, set 3 to 4-inch sections 2 inches deep and 2 inches apart in sand or sandy soil.

Although tip cuttings are preferable, you can also use older stems, which are usually more woody at the base.

DIVISIONS AND OTHER METHODS

Any succulent that forms clumps, such as the echeveria, can be divided. Each rosette will start a new clump. Plant the rosette so its base is level with the surface of the soil.

Sempervivum and similar rosette-like succulents produce offsets, or tiny replicas of themselves, all around their base. If removed and planted, each offset becomes the nucleus of its own ring of offsets.

On bryophyllums and kalanchoes, look for little plantlets growing on the margins of the leaves. You can

remove these proliferations and start them in flats or pots.

It's no trick to root leaves of many succulents—simply stick the lower ends in sand or soil. But you won't get a full sized plant as quickly as from the other methods described above.

When making cuttings of succulents, let them dry out for a few days to reduce the amount of water in their stems and leaves. They will then be less likely to rot.

GROWING SUCCULENTS FROM SEED

Most succulents grow from seed as readily as annuals and perennials do. Since you don't need elaborate equipment, and the cost of seed is low compared with the price of nursery plants, you can start a varied succulent collection by investing no more than a dollar or two. In fact, if you want some of the rarer types, you can get them only by growing the seed.

Many seed companies and nurseries which specialize in succulents and cactus offer seed collections for as little as 25 cents. Most packets contain seed of at least 10

LEFT. *From these leaves new succulents will grow.* Bryophyllum, *top left;* echeveria, *top and middle right; others are sedum leaves. All root readily in damp sand.* CENTER. *Mexican sedum cuttings. Clockwise from* *planted flat: long cuttings to plant out; short ones to start in flat; rooted plants; older rooted stems.* RIGHT. *Clump, divisions of* Echeveria elegans, *a typical clump-forming succulent. Divisions form solid mass in year.*

different species and varieties. Some succulent specialists offer packets containing as many as 75.

October is as good a month as any to start succulent seed indoors, especially if you can provide a warm, even room temperature of about 72°. Under good conditions many seeds will germinate in about one week; others may take a month or two. Although a frame with bottom heat of 75° to 85° is ideal, it's not absolutely necessary. If you build a device like the one illustrated, you can even grow your seed outside in a lathhouse.

For succulent seed—a porous, well drained soil

Although growers differ slightly on what soil mixture is best for starting succulent seeds, formula below has been found highly satisfactory:

     5 parts clean, sharp river sand
     2 parts thoroughly rotted leaf mold, screened
     2 parts light garden soil
     1 part powdered charcoal

Sift the soil mixture through a ¼-inch mesh screen. (NOTE: *While you are at it, make up a large amount so you can store part to use as a medium for the seedlings you will transplant at a later date.*)

Sterilize soil to insure healthy seedlings

To prevent damping-off, it's a good idea to sterilize the soil mixture. Damping-off is caused by a fungus that grows in most soils and attacks germinating seeds or the stems of small seedlings at the soil level. The disease is most active under conditions of constant moisture and poor air circulation.

Probably the easiest method of sterilizing the soil is to heat it in a 300° oven for about 30 minutes or until all the moisture is driven off. You can also place pots of soil on a frame in a pressure cooker, with ½ inch of water on the bottom and steam for 5 to 10 minutes. Or set them in a large covered kettle containing ½ inch of water and boil them about 30 minutes.

If you don't want to sterilize the soil by one of these methods, you can prevent damping-off by treating the seed or soil with one of the commercial fungicides available for the purpose.

Type of containers to use

Shallow clay pots or fern pans 4 to 6 inches in diameter make the best containers for starting seeds. However, almost any clay pot or can with drainage holes in the bottom is good.

Place about a 1-inch layer of broken pots or crockery in the bottom of the container. (One grower suggests substituting coarse charcoal for the crocks.) Add the sifted soil mix to within about 1 inch of the top of the container.

Seeds are small—plant carefully

Using tweezers, carefully plant seed, scar side down. (A magnifying glass comes in very handy in this operation.) Deep planting is usually fatal. Insert seeds just below the soil surface, and space them about ½ to 1 inch apart. Sprinkle a very light layer of fine sand or powdered charcoal over the seed.

Water the pots from below. Set them in a pail of tepid water until the soil surface is moist. Remove the pots, allow excess water to drain, and place them in a well lighted frame or window protected from direct sunlight. Cover the pots with a pane of glass and place a sheet of newspaper on top.

If the glass fogs heavily, turn it over and wipe off the excess moisture. You'll probably have to do this every day.

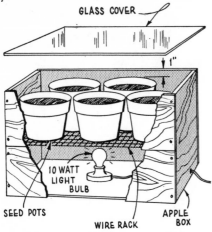

As seeds begin to germinate, tear holes in the paper to allow more light to reach the seedlings. To increase air circulation, place a wooden match under the edge of

the glass. Do not remove the glass until all seeds are up, but increase the amount of ventilation as the seedlings grow. Continue to water from below, but don't let the soil get too wet—extremes of either wetness or dryness may kill the young seedlings.

Transplanting the small seedlings

Transplant seedlings into small pots when they're large enough to handle without tearing the roots. You can move seedlings of many types of succulents when they're only ¼ inch high. If you don't have a suitable lifting tool, a plant label or tongue depressor with a V-notch on one end works admirably. If seedlings are too crowded to move individually without injuring them, transplant small clumps and separate them when they're larger.

For the transplanted seedlings, use the soil mix you prepared for the seeds; but in each two or three gallons of soil, mix an additional part of leaf mold and one pound of bonemeal. Don't forget to provide the new containers with adequate drainage, as described.

LEFT: *Plant various kinds of seeds in one container. Mark with plant labels.* CENTER: *When seedlings large enough to handle, move into 1½-inch pots.* RIGHT: *Tiny cotyledon seedlings are ready to transplant.*

In the Swiss-style French casserole are seven herbs growing in three-inch pots. As keyed in plan, they are: (1) dwarf lavender, (2) pot marjoram, (3) common thyme, (4) rosemary, (5) sage, (6) peppermint, and (7) winter savory.

HERBS-VEGETABLES: A COMPACT FOOD GARDEN AT YOUR KITCHEN DOOR

If you have a small garden, or even if you have a large one, it's a good idea to grow a half dozen or so herbs in a box, tub, or group of pots on your terrace or near your kitchen door.

Redwood or cedar boxes, flue tiles, strawberry jars, or pots make handsome containers for herbs. Those that are portable can be moved around to suit tne time and situation. Container-grown herbs that lose their leaves in winter can be moved to an out-of-the-way corner of the garden during their dormant period. Culinary herbs can be placed near the barbecue in summer, near the kitchen in winter.

When herbs with different habits, and possibly different cultural needs, are grown in one container or near each other, it is helpful to separate them with solid divisions of wood, metal, or some other impenetrable material. Thus, invasive roots of some plants are prevented from encroaching on those of neighboring plants and it is possible to give to each plant the varying amounts of water they require.

Shown here are planting suggestions for a redwood box with several partitions, and a tub divided into quarters.

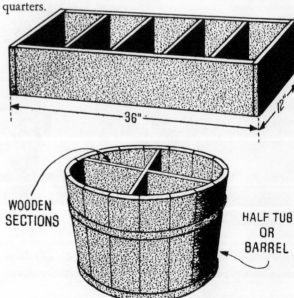

36"

12"

WOODEN SECTIONS

HALF TUB OR BARREL

Herb box near kitchen has parsley, rosemary, chives, mint, tarragon. Box of redwood with mitered corners.

PLANTING SUGGESTIONS

Almost any herb may be grown in a container. The following are particularly good:

Chives *(Allium schoenoprasum)*. A 1-foot-high perennial. Compact; grass-like leaves; lavender flowers in spherical clusters above leaves. Use freshly picked. *Culture.* Full sun; partial shade in hot interior valleys. Rich soil, ample moisture. Cut frequently to keep flowers from

In planter near front door, handsome dwarf rosemary offers a fragrant welcome. Blue flowers in winter.

forming and leaves from hardening. If cut back more than two-thirds, a plant will die. Fertilize after cutting with liquid feed to stimulate new growth. Divide clumps every 3 years. Propagate from seeds or divisions.

Chervil *(Anthriscus cerefolium)*. Annual to 2 feet tall. Fine-cut, fern-like leaf resembling parsley; white flower. Use fresh from the garden. *Culture.* Partial shade, ordinary garden soils, average moisture. Grow from seed.

In containers: tender herbs to move indoors in winter, invasive ones that need confining, patio display plants.

Close to the kitchen, grow your favorite cooking herbs —parsley, chives, thyme, mint, marjoram and rosemary.

Herb lineup: (1) Golden apple mint. (2) Orange mint. (3) Lemon verbena is nice at corner of path where you

are sure to brush against it. (4) Garden sage, dramatic container plant, is useful kitchen herb, fresh or dry.

Costmary *(Chrysanthemum balsamita).* Perennial to 3 feet tall. Loose and spreading, with gray-green toothed leaves, small yellow button flowers. Use in tea, salads, potpourris. *Culture.* Sun or shade; dry soil. Thin frequently by pulling up rooted stems. Costmary spreads rapidly. You can keep it to 8 to 10 inches high by pruning back vigorously. Divide every 3 years.

English lavender *(Lavandula officinalis).* Shrub to 3 to 6 feet tall. Narrow, gray-green leaves; light lavender flowers in spikes. French lavender *(L. dentata)* grows to 4 feet. Bloom is almost continuous. It is less fragrant than English lavender. Handsome with pink dianthus. Use in sachets. *Culture.* Sun; will take some shade; light sandy soil, on the dry side. If not pruned hard after flowering, it gets woody. Replant every 4 years.

Lemon verbena *(Lippia citriodora).* A 3 to 12-foot-high shrub. Long, narrow, green leaves; white flowers in spikes or panicles. Mix with lavender in sachets; use in apple jelly. *Culture.* Sun, average soil and moisture. Keep it pruned during the growing season. Protect from frost in winter. Lemon verbena is tender. Propagate from cuttings and seed.

Sweet marjoram *(Majorana hortensis).* Perennial to 2 feet tall, treated as annual in cold winter areas. Tiny gray-green leaves; white flowers in knotted clusters. Use leaves fresh or dried. *Culture.* Full sun, fairly moist soil. Keep blossoms cut off and plant trimmed to prevent woody growth. Propagate from seed, cuttings, or root divisions.

Orange mint, bergamot mint *(Mentha citrata).* Perennial to 2 feet tall. Dark green leaves; small lavender flowers. Use like other mints. Slight orange-like flavor. *Culture.* Part shade; light, medium rich soil; moist conditions. Keep flowers cut off. Replant every 3 years.

Golden apple mint *(Mentha gentilis).* Perennial to 2 feet tall. Smooth, deep green leaves, variegated yellow. Use like other mints. *Culture.* Partial shade;

Spearmint *(Mentha spicata).* Perennial 18 to 24 inches tall. Dark green leaves; leafy spikes of purplish flowers. Use fresh from the garden. *Culture.* Full sun or partial shade. With adequate moisture spreads rapidly by underground stems. Propagate from runners.

Basil *(Ocimum basilicum).* Annual to 2 inches high. Medium sized leaves, sometimes purplish; white or purplish flowers. Use fresh or dried. *Culture.* Sun, average moisture, light and well drained soil. Plant seeds each month for a steady supply of basil. Pinch out tips to keep plant bushy. Keep flowers cut. Plant will produce two crops a year.

Oregano, wild marjoram *(Origanum vulgare).* Hardy perennial to 2½ feet tall. Medium sized, oval leaves; purplish pink blooms. Although oregano is best fresh, you can use it dried. *Culture.* Sun, medium rich soil, good drainage, average watering. Keep trimmed to prevent flowering. Replant every 3 years.

Parsley *(Petroselinum crispum).* A 2 to 10-inch-high biennial, usually treated as an annual. Dark green, tightly curled leaves. Slow growing. Use fresh or dried. *Culture.* Sun, good soil, average watering. Buy plants at a nursery, or plant in place from seed. Soak seed in warm water 24 hours before planting. Sow seeds a few inches apart. Don't let plant go to seed.

Prostrate rosemary *(Rosmarinus officinalis prostratus).* Spreading form of the common rosemary. Not over 15 inches high. Dark green, needle-like leaves; light blue flowers. *R.o.* Lockwood de Forest has lighter green foliage and deeper blue flowers. Use in sachets. *Culture:* Full sun, well drained gravelly soil slightly on the lean side. Drought resistant.

Garden sage *(Salvia officinalis)*. Perennial 18 to 24 inches high. Gray leaves; spikes of violet blue flowers. Use fresh or dry. *Culture.* Sun, poor soil. Fairly drought resistant. Cut it back after bloom. Fertilize if you cut it continually. Divide every 3 to 4 years. Propagate from cuttings, layers, or seed to increase your plants.

Small burnet *(Sanguisorba minor)*. Perennial 8 to 12 inches tall. Deeply toothed leaflets arranged along the stems, producing a lacy pattern; small, inconspicuous flowers. Use in salads for slight cucumber flavor, also in vinegar. *Culture.* Sun, poor soil, adequate moisture. Keep blossoms cut. Don't cut back plant more than half. Do not place pot near garden bed because small burnet self-seeds almost too freely.

Common thyme *(Thymus vulgaris)*. Perennial to 8 inches high. Small, green leaves; tiny lavender flowers. It is useful fresh or dried. *Culture.* Sun; light, sandy soil that is moderately dry. Prune after flowering. Replant every 3 years. Propagate from cuttings taken early in summer, before flowering, or from seed.

VEGETABLES IN CONTAINERS

Besides being edible, there are a number of vegetables that are ornamental as well. Here are a few you might try in containers—possibly along with some of the herbs:

Artichokes. Mounds of blue-green, coarsely cut and lobed leaves, globular flower buds which can be cut and cooked as a vegetable or left to develop into the lavender thistle-like bloom. Flower very ornamental in arrangements. Green Globe variety most popular in the West. *Culture.* Plant in a large container, otherwise they may not produce eating-size artichokes. Set out offshoots or divisions in fall or winter, keeping crowns above soil level. Water deeply. Harvest artichokes between November and June when 2 to 4 inches in diameter, before bracts start to open. After harvest, cut out old part of plant to make way for new side shoots. Mulch the soil with manure. Replace with new plants about every 4 to 7 years.

Flowering kale. In seedling stage looks like any other kale, but as it matures, rosette of leaves turn from white or cream to pink, rose, and magenta on background of green. Colors become more brilliant as season advances. *Culture.* Sow seed in July for color in early September. Seed takes about 10 days to germinate.

Peppers. Upright growth, attractive foliage, handsome shiny green and red fruits. Fruits vary in size with type; mild Bell pepper has largest fruits; chili peppers, long narrow fruits; cayenne, narrow often curled and twisted fruit. *Culture.* Buy seedlings of standard varieties at local nurseries; grow unusual types from seed. Keep soil moist. Fertilize once or twice between planting time and blossom set to keep plants growing vigorously.

Rhubarb chard. Strong, erect, translucent scarlet leaf stalks, rich green crinkly leaves deeply veined in red. *Culture.* Sow seed up to July 1 for harvest before frost.

Small fruited tomatoes. Plants same size as large fruited varieties, fruits miniature, but in large clusters. Included in this group: grape tomato (sometimes called red currant or raisin tomato), very sweet, small fruit in grape-like clusters; cherry tomato, slightly larger, like sweet cherry, red and yellow varieties; plum tomato, blander, larger, less juicy, slightly elongated, yellow or red; pear tomato, egg-sized, pear shaped, yellow and red varieties, waxy skin. *Culture.* Set plants outdoors after danger of frost. In containers, handsome trained on trellis as espalier. Check pots daily, don't let soil dry out.

(5.) Sweet marjoram, a must in herb garden; use both fresh and dried. (6.) Oregano, another useful kitchen *herb, grows in soft gray mounds. (7.) Chives, primarily associated with kitchen effective with thyme.*

Here's a novel table centerpiece. "Mountains" are lightweight volcanic rock. Kept on covered terrace, but brought inside (a 2-man job) on special occasions. Here is a list of the plants: Jelecote pine (Pinus patula), *silverberry* (Elaeagnus pungens), Calocaphalus brownii, *mother of thyme* (Thymus serpyllum), *woolly thyme* (T. s. lanuginosus), *winter savory* (Satureja montana), *and Corsican sandwort* (Arenaria balearica).

MINIATURES: NO PLANT, NO CONTAINER TOO SMALL FOR A MINIATURE GARDEN

A miniature landscape can take form in almost any kind of container—from a large planter to a teacup shown on the next page. If you're a gardener, you can fashion landscapes complete with mountains, rocky valleys, and living plants for trees. Or perhaps you want the effect of a single plant. If you're not a gardener, you don't need plants at all; just use rocks, pebbles, and figurines.

The landscapes you see here give an idea of what can be done easily and inexpensively. Look around the house and you'll probably turn up several suitable containers. If you decide to buy one, you can find some very handsome containers for $2 or less. Small rocks and pebbles are available near rivers and beaches, of course, and

nurseries can supply the "trees" for your landscape.

If you use plants, put them in a loose soil mixture (see section on potting mixtures). Containers should have about an inch of crushed gravel in the bottom for drainage. It isn't necessary to have drain holes in the container if you are careful not to overwater.

Outdoor plants such as those used in the large planting box won't grow for long inside, but will thrive outside in a patio or on a terrace.

Perhaps the most satisfying miniature garden is one that includes a small tree or shrub, and a few perennials, annuals, or bulbs, and possibly a ground cover. With

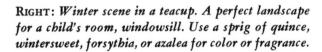

Oriental scene in a wooden rice tub. Dominant plant is mistletoe fig (Ficus diversifolia); the other plant is mondo grass. Kokeshi doll, lantern add touch of color.

This arrangement costs about $5 (including bowl). Ducks, figurine stand on the edge of a pocket mirror pool in the shade of a variegated Chlorophytum elatum.

RIGHT: *Winter scene in a teacup. A perfect landscape for a child's room, windowsill. Use a sprig of quince, wintersweet, forsythia, or azalea for color or fragrance.*

this variety of materials, accessories are unnecessary.

Following are a few of the miniature species and varieties available in specialty nurseries. For descriptions of these plants, see the *Sunset Western Garden Book*.

CONIFERS

Chamaecyparis pisifera pygmaea, dwarf Hinoki cypress *(C. obtusa nana); Cryptomeria japonica nana;* dwarf juniper *(Juniperus communis compressa); Picea abies procumbens, P. a. nidiformis, P. glauca conica;* Tom Thumb arborvitae *(Thuja occidentalis globosa),* Berckmann's arborvitae *(T. orientalis nana).*

SHRUBLETS

Prostrate broom *(Cytisus decumbens); Cotoneaster* Tom Thumb; heather *(Calluna vulgaris foxii nana, C. vulgaris nana); Pieris nana;* lingonberry *(Vaccinium vitisidaea).*

PERENNIALS

Ajuga metallica crispa; Armeria juniperifolia; bellflowers *Campanula portenschlagiana, C. elatines garganica, C. carpatica;* small forms of *Dianthus;* evergreen candytuft *(Iberis sempervirens);* dwarf iris; dwarf geraniums.

RIGHT: *Sushi tray makes a handsome container for a beach scene with white stones, sand, bleached coral. At night a candle burns cheerfully in the tiny lantern.*

ERNEST BRAUN

Elaeagnus with yellow-centered leaves, arches over small juniper and a mossy rock. Restricted root space, plus occasional pinching will keep plants in proper scale with container.

SHRUBS—TREES: ESSENTIAL BACKGROUND FOR AN OUTDOOR CONTAINER GARDEN

Shrubs and trees are basic plants in containers just as they are out in the garden. Evergreen species give you all-year effects and furnish backgrounds for displays of seasonal color.

Almost any shrub or tree can be grown in a container. Generally, dwarf or slow-growing plants are most satisfactory because they don't require re-potting as often and remain in better scale with the container. With occasional root pruning and renewal of the potting mixture, some shrubs and trees can live comfortably in the same container for scores of years. Bonsais, of course, are classic examples (see page 70). Here, however, we are not concerned with this special class of plants, but with shrubs and trees that are normally planted in the garden.

WHEN AND HOW TO PLANT

An important advantage of growing shrubs and trees in containers is that you can plant them at any time they are available. Now that more and more nurseries carry material in cans, you can plant even the deciduous kinds (once usually sold bare root in their dormant season) the year around.

In desert areas, it is hazardous to plant during hot weather unless you carefully shade and water newly planted material. Spraying leaves of these plants with water one or two times a day on summer days helps to reduce transpiration.

Set the plant so that the surface of the soil is at least 2 inches below the rim of the container. In larger containers, 3 inches is even better. This will allow ample space for watering as well as for a mulch of peat moss or other humous material, or pebbles, gravel, or a plant ground cover. It's especially important to provide for deep watering in hot summer climates.

Because soil in containers warms up and dries out faster than soil in the open ground, most container plants —even the sun-loving kinds like citrus and hibiscus—do better if you keep them in filtered light in hot weather. This is invariably so in the desert and other warm inland areas.

White azalea makes elegant feature near entry. Pot aza-leas in pure peat or peat and sand; re-pot every 2 or 3 years. After bloom feed with acid-base fertilizer.

Galvanized wash tubs, 20½ inches square, painted dark green. Punch holes for drainage; stand on cleats. Plants: pelargoniums, geraniums, purple heliotrope.

WATERING AND FERTILIZING

There is no set rule for watering and fertilizing that applies to all trees and shrubs in containers. The amount of water and the frequency with which you apply it depends on the kind of plant, the size and kind of container, the soil mix, your climate, the exposure in which the container is placed, whether or not you use a mulch, and the nature and depth of the mulch. Using a soil moisture measuring device is the only accurate way of determining when a plant needs water, but few gardeners own this instrument. Next best way to know when to water your plants is to watch them closely and to test the soil. If leaves start looking limp, or if you can't easily push a ¼-inch metal rod or small wooden stake into the soil, it's time to water.

If you use one of the U.C.-type soil mixes, it is prac-tically impossible to overwater because these mixes permit excellent drainage.

There are several balanced fertilizers on the market that are recommended for feeding shrubs and trees. All manufacturers' labels carry directions that specify amounts and timing of fertilizer applications; be sure to follow these directions.

SHRUBS FOR CONTAINERS

Abelia grandiflora, dwarf form (sometimes called *A. g. prostrata*). A low mounding variety of the taller species. Small, bright evergreen, glossy foliage. Clusters of white

to pale pink, delicately fragrant flowers cover the flat branches from July to October. Bright colored sepals persist after blossoms have fallen, giving the effect of continued bloom. Hardy to 15°.

Strawberry tree *(Arbutus unedo).* Rangy, thick shrub which can be trained as a tree. Moderate growth, will reach about 6 to 8 feet in a 2-foot-square container. White to greenish flowers all year followed by red and yellow warty fruits in all except colder areas. Hardy to 15°.

Greenleaf aucuba *(A. japonica).* Moderate growth from 5 to 6 feet high in a large container, often to 5 feet wide, forming an irregular, bulky, informal shrub. Clean, thickish, lush green, 7-inch leaves ovate or oblong, and coarsely toothed. Tiny dark maroon flowers in March, followed by clusters of bright red, ¾-inch berries from October to February. Because fruit is borne on female plants only, both sexes must be planted to insure a fruit crop. Hardy to 15°.

Azaleas. Although there are many species and varie-ties of azaleas, the Belgian Indicas and Kurumes are probably best adapted to container culture. Belgian In-dicas and Belgian Indica Hybrids are the least hardy of the evergreen azaleas—suffer from bark splitting when temperatures drop below 20°. The large double-flowered varieties come in particularly bright colors, show off beautifully in tubs.

Indicas, the compact types grow to 3 to 5 feet in 10 years; taller growers go to 6 to 8 feet. Flowers are smaller and never as double as the Belgian Indicas, but quantity of bloom makes up for smaller size. Season of bloom is from March to May.

Bamboos. Give light yellow-green airy effect. Two kinds well adapted to tubs: **Golden bamboo** (*Phyllostachys aurea*), 8 to 10 feet high in a container, hardy to 20°; **hedge bamboo** (*Bambusa multiplex*), available in several different forms, including Alphonse Karr, 12 to 15 feet high; Chinese Goddess, 4 to 6 feet high; hardy to 20°; new culms and branches bright pinkish-yellow changing to golden yellow with longitudinal green stripes of differing widths irregularly spaced on internodes.

Camellia japonica. Dense, usually dark green, glossy foliage. Profusion of flowers. Many colors and heights, depending on variety. Hardy to 15°. (See the *Sunset* Book, *How to Grow Camellias.*)

Natal plum (*Carissa*). *C. grandiflora*, evergreen rounded shrub of loose growth habit generally grows to 3 to 5 feet in a container. Leaves ovate to 3 inches long; flowers white, 2 inches across, appear throughout the year. Fruit, a red plum 1 to 2 inches long. For best fruit production grow more than one plant for cross pollination. Hardy to 20°, foliage damaged at 26°. The variety

C. g. prostrata, a seedling of *C. grandiflora*, has low horizontal growth, forms a glossy mound of foliage which spills gracefully over the side of a container. 1½ to 2 feet high.

Hinoki false cypress (*Chamaecyparis obtusa*). Generally pyramidal in habit, 4 to 6 feet. Very slow growing, often treated as dwarf and trained and shaped to emphasize its irregular branching habit. Hardy to about 10°. *C. o. nana*, an upright, round headed tree to 3 to 5 feet with deep green foliage in flat, stratified planes, smooth reddish-brown bark that peels in thin strips. *C. o. ericoides*, a round-headed variety to 4 to 6 feet, has fluffy gray-green foliage which turns purple-brown in winter.

Silverberry (*Elaeagnus pungens*). Slow growing, rather sprawling shrub. Keep compact by pruning. Gray-green foliage that glistens in sun. Also interesting and unusual variegated forms. Hardy to 15°.

Japanese fatsia (*Fatsia japonica*). Tropical-looking shrub with rapid growth to 4 to 6 feet with a wide spread. Bold, fan-shaped, deeply lobed leaves, dark glossy green. Hardy to 15°.

Pineapple guava (*Feijoa sellowiana*). Moderate growth to 6 to 8 feet in a container. Oval leaves, 2 to 3 inches long are gray-green above, silvery white beneath. Exotic 1-inch flowers with white fleshy petals, purplish inside; many showy dark red stamens, from May to July. Edible gray-green fruits. One of the more hardy of the subtropicals—temperatures to 20° without damage.

Fuchsias. This popular plant is available in many colors. Bushy and upright forms with flowers in many colors. Bell-shaped flowers all summer. Hardy to 20°.

Citrus. Most kinds of dwarf citrus are superb container subjects. Their glossy evergreen foliage, fragrant bloom, and colorful fruit make them ideal for terrace or patio in mild-winter climates, and they can also be grown indoors with extra care and attention.

Orange. Robertson Navel—early, heavy bearing; Shamoudi—midwinter bearing.

Mandarin orange. Kinnow—excellent spring-ripened fruit; Clementine (Algerian) mandarin—January ripening.

Lemon. Eureka—year-round fruit; Ponderosa—large (12-inch circumference) fruit most of the year.

Lime. Bearss Seedless—main bearing season in spring.

Tangelo. Sampson—fruit from late spring to summer.

Kumquat. Nagami—olive-sized fruit in late fall.

Large box holds combination of plants in varying textures and leaf colors. Bamboo won't intrude if the roots are confined in can or pot, or are separated by metal.

Gardenia. Evergreen, slow to moderate growth. *G. jasminoides* grows luxuriantly to 4 to 6 feet with regular branching habit and glossy green foliage. Extremely fragrant, waxy-white single and semi-double flowers in summer. Variety *Mystery* is typical of the species. Variety *Veitchi* has smaller flowers in greater profusion, and smaller leaves. Hardy to 20°.

Gunnera chilensis. Extremely fast-growing evergreen plant suggestive of giant rhubarb. Deeply lobed and cut leaves 3 to 4 feet in diameter on fleshy, stiff-hairy stalks to 4 feet or more long in containers. Comparatively small, colorless flowers in 3-foot spikes, red fruits and seeds in corncob-like structure. Needs constant water to attain size. Hardy to 30°.

Chinese hibiscus *(H. rosa-sinensis).* Rather open, 5 to 6-foot shrub, slow to become established, slow to recover when hit by frost. Dark green, glossy foliage. Many, many varieties offer either single or double, 6-inch broad flowers in wide range of colors—pale yellow to amber, white and shell pink to rose, bright vermilion. Hardy to 30°.

Bigleaf hydrangea *(H. macrophylla,* sometimes sold as *H. hortensia* or *H. opuloides).* Hardy, deciduous shrub, symmetrical growth to 6 feet with thick, shining, broadly ovate, 8-inch leaves. Blue, pink, or white flowers in flattish or rounded 6 to 8-inch clusters. French hybrids extend the color range to rose, carmine, red, deep blue, violet, and snow white.

Holly *(Ilex).* Evergreen shrub which includes familiar English holly as well as many obscure cousins from foot-high sprawling shrubs to tall trees. The slow-growing hollies usually need a male plant (pollenizer) to insure a crop of berries on the female plant. Grafted stock is also available; certain species are infertile.

English holly *(I. aquifolium).* Traditional Christmas holly. Slow growing to 8 feet in containers. Flowers in May and June followed by scarlet berries. Many

BLAIR STAPP

THEODORE OSMUNDSON

TOP: *A good shrub for container growing is the willowy, fall blooming Camellia sasanqua, here trained on trellis.*

CENTER: *Hibiscus perform very well in adequately sized tubs. Produce striking blooms throughout summer. Tender.*

BOTTOM: *Large clusters of pink, rose, or blue flowers, and lustrous green leaves make the hydrangea a most satisfactory summer tub shrub. Vigorous grower, needs big tub.*

Pineapple guava looks handsome in brown-stained box. Redwood lath in vertical lap, nailed to 1 by 12's, repeats fence siding. Brown color contrasts with foliage.

Three ginkgos in cast concrete container at the end of pierced concrete block wall. Slow growing trees such as these can be kept in a container for several seasons.

horticultural forms both green leafed and variegated. Hardy, but best where temperatures don't go below 15°.

Chinese holly *(I. cornuta)*. Resembles English holly, but lower growing. Leaves have fewer spines. Will set berries without pollenizer. Fruits heavily with big, scarlet berries at Christmas time. Hardy to 20°.

Broad-leafed holly *(I. altaclarensis wilsonii)*. Grows 6 to 8 feet. Resembles green-leafed English form, but on a larger scale, with leaves 3 to 4 inches long.

Japanese holly *(I. crenata)*. Shrub to 6 feet with dark green foliage, black berries. Variety *helleri,* dwarf from 6 to 8 inches.

Juniper *(Juniperus)*. Hardy evergreen. Low prostrate forms particularly adaptable for container gardening. Junipers have two kinds of leaves on their branches—scale-like, which make branches look like braided cords; needle-like, which give them a fine-textured look. Some of the more common junipers have both textures on one plant, which also give a fine-textured effect.

J. chinensis armstrongii. Looks like a small Pfitzer juniper. Low, arching habit to 2 feet. Has both scale-like and needle-like leaves.

Shore juniper *(J. conferta)*. Forms a low, 1 to 2-foot, uneven mat of blue-green foliage. Leaves all needle-like. A natural with stone.

Creeping juniper *(J. horizontalis)*. Prostrate, creeping shrub to 18 inches, forms compact mat of blue-gray foliage.

Tamarix juniper *(J. sabina tamariscifolia)*. To 2 feet high, but wide spreading. Sprays of rather fine, bright green leaves—both scale-like and needle-like. A variegated form has occasional branches dappled creamy-white.

Twisted juniper *(J. chinensis torulosa)*. Interesting, narrow, columnar form to 6 to 8 feet, with open, twisting branches. Dark green foliage of scale-like leaves. A variegated form has tips of branches splashed with creamy-white.

Trailing lantanas (forms of *Lantana camara*). Evergreen, or deciduous in cold weather. Moonglow: vigorous, low, spreading growth habit; soft, yellow flowers. Copper Lustre: bronze, coppery flowers. Hardy to 24°.

English lavender *(Lavandula officinalis)*. Evergreen shrub to 2 to 3 feet. Narrow, gray, long leaves. Fragrant, light lavendar flower spikes in summer. Hardy

Loropetalum chinense. Picturesque evergreen shrub. Varying heights: to 3 feet in short-season climates, to 10 feet in warm areas. Good show of downy-white to cream, delicate, 1-inch flowers in spring and early summer. Light green, pointed, 2-inch leaves. Hardy to 15°.

ERNEST BRAUN

Hexagonal redwood tub 18 inches in diameter and 16½ inches high holds Magnolia. Slow growing trees make ideal container subjects; can stay in a tub for years.

Wood and bamboo soy tub 14 inches in diameter is compatible with variegated aralia. Soy tubs can be obtained from oriental importers, nurseries, basket shops.

Mahonia. Evergreen. *M. bealei,* a hardy tree-like shrub to 6 feet. Flat whorls of branches grow horizontally from an erect trunk. Gray-green leaves of 9 to 15 ovate, 5-inch leaflets with stiff, spiny teeth on the margins. Clusters of yellow flowers in spring followed by bluish berries. *M. lomarifolia,* when young, is a single stemmed vertical plant to 6 to 8 feet; as plant matures forms multiple trunks and becomes shrub 10 to 12 feet. Leaves of 21 to 29 rather narrow, thick, spiny leaflets. Clusters of yellow flowers in early spring followed by bluish berries.

Banana shrub (*Michelia fuscata*). Evergreen shrub 4 to 6 feet high, with deep green, lustrous, oblong leaves to 3 inches long. Flowers, opening in March resembling small magnolia blossoms, are 1½ inches across, creamy-yellow with purple or brownish shading. Bloom for a month or more, with rich banana-like fragrance. Hardy to 25°.

Heavenly bamboo (*Nandina domestica*). Slow growing evergreen to 3 to 5 feet. Semi-deciduous in cold winters—loses its leaves at 10°; killed to the ground at 5°. Light airy structure pattern of slender, unbranched, cane-like stems and fine-textured, delicate, much divided leaves. New leaves tinged pink and bronzy-red, turn soft light green as they mature, pick up purple bronze tints in fall, and often turn a fiery crimson in winter. Flowers in loose, erect, 12-inch clusters of creamy white or pink in late spring; shiny red berries in fall.

ROBERT COX

Triangular boxes in front of reed screen are planted with golden bamboo. Boxes have strong design quality, restrict plant roots. Bamboo repeats pattern of the reed.

Weeping copper beech in 12-inch blue glazed Japanese Shigaraki pot. This is natural form of this rare tree. It has been potted in the same container for about 2 years.

Large Japanese soy tub is in good scale with tall slender plants. With more growth, however, this Podocarpus macrophylla *will be in better proportion with the tub.*

Oleander *(Nerium oleander).* Evergreen, moderate growth to 6 to 8 feet in a container. Normally grows as a many stemmed, many-branched shrub, but can be trained as single multiple-trunked tree. Foliage of dark green, long, narrow, 5 to 8-inch leaves. Flowers, 2 to 3 inches across, in profusion from May or June to October. Single and double-flowered varieties in shades of white, light pink, salmon-pink, deep rose, red, and light yellow. Hardy to 20°.

New Zealand flax *(Phormium tenax).* Evergreen, 4 to 6 feet tall in containers. Sword-like, stiffly vertical leaves arranged in fan pattern become dense clumps spreading to 6 feet or more. Reddish-brown stalks that tower above the leaves bear curiously shaped dark red to yellowish flowers in spring. Hardy to 20°.

Varieties available in different heights, foliage color, leaf width, and rate of growth. Common all-green form; others with gray-green leaves with red midrib; green edged with white or yellow; also come with greenish-bronze and dark red leaves, and with narrow 4-foot-long leaves.

Pieris. Slow growing shrubs with year-around interest. Hardy.

Lily-of-the-valley shrub *(P. japonica).* Rather open shrub 3 to 5 feet when mature. Lustrous, dark green, pointed, 3-inch leaves held in graceful radial clusters.

New foliage in spring bronzy pink to scarlet. In fall delicate strands of greenish-pink buds hang from tips of branches, fatten during winter, and in very early spring open into pearly white, urn-shaped flowers.

P. floribunda. More compact and rounded to 2 to 3 feet high and 4 to 6 feet wide. Longer leaves. Spikes of flowers held upright rather than drooping.

Tobira, Japanese pittosporum *(P. tobira).* Spreading shrub 4 to 6 feet, can be held back by selective pruning of stems. Leathery, dark green, 4-inch leaves. Clusters of creamy-white flowers with orange-blossom fragrance. Brownish fruits. Hardy to 15°.

P. t. variegata. Growth can be held to 5 feet. Gray-green leaves outlined in white.

Fern pine *(Podocarpus elongata).* Evergreen conifer, easy to train, especially when young. Irregular structure to 15 feet, can be kept to 8 feet in tub. Graceful, rather pendulous branches with dark green, soft, willowy leaves. Hardy to 10°.

Yew pine *(P. macrophylla).* Slower growing than *P. elongata.* Similar to the above, but foliage lighter green, leaves wider.

Strawberry guava *(Psidium cattleianum).* Large, open shrub, moderately growing to 6 to 8 feet or sometimes an excellent small tree to 15 feet, lower in containers. Glossy, dark green, bronze-tipped, 3-inch leaves. White, 1-inch flowers with many stamens, resemble

This dwarf Eureka lemon is 3½ years old and about 3½ feet tall. Note that it is more tree-like than most citrus. Lemon can be pruned more easily than orange.

Dwarf Eustis limequat bears year around in mild climate areas. Sensitive to frost. This plant set in mix of half topsoil, half peat, mulched with white gravel.

those of common myrtle. Flowers followed by 1½-inch deep, claret red fruits. Hardy to 15°.

   Dwarf pomegranate *(Punica granatum nana).* Deciduous shrub to 3 feet (almost evergreen in mild climates). Bushy, compact, well mannered. Bears fruit

when no more than 12 inches tall. Tiny orange fruits are dry and not edible. Double flowered forms and several color variations from yellow to orange. As a container plant, can progressively move from 6-inch pot to a 14-inch box in about 5 years. Hardy to about 20°.

LEFT. *Dancy tangerines can be colorful with fruit all year because fruit stores well on tree.* RIGHT. *Kinnow mandarin makes rounded tree with attractive, dense willow-like leaves. Fine-flavored fruit in alternate years.*

MORLEY BAER   DARROW M. WATT

LEFT: Tub rests on dolly so it can be pushed over smooth concrete terrace. Loquat tree is the prominent plant in the container; trailing rosemary and lobelia at *base. CENTER. Redwood box of 2-inch material contains Japanese maple. RIGHT: Cement block with added one-inch base designed for dwarf deodar cedar.*

Roses. Floribunda or polyantha roses generally best suited to container culture because bushy compact growth and continual abundance of bloom from spring through fall. Countless varieties ranging in color from white to shades of yellow, pink, red, and white. (See the *Sunset* Book, *How to Grow Roses.*)

Common rosemary *(Rosmarinus officinalis)*. Evergreen shrub that will reach 6 feet, but can be kept to 4 feet. Narrow, aromatic leaves glossy, dark green above, gray-white beneath. Small clusters of light lavender-blue, ½-inch flowers in winter and spring. Variety Heavenly Blue, an improved form, grows into a roundish shrub 2 to 3 feet high with semi-trailing branches. Flowers are truer blue than the species. *R. o. prostratus* stays under 24 inches, spreads to 4 or more feet wide if given space. Dark green narrow leaves, light blue flowers in April and May. *R. o. Lockwood De Forest* has lighter bright green foliage, bluer flowers. Hardy to about 15°.

Queensland umbrella tree *(Brassaia actinophylla* often sold as *Schefflera actinophylla)*. Treated as indoor plant where temperatures drop below 30°. Fast growing tropical to 20 feet. Horizontal tiers of glittering bright green compound leaves of 6 to 8 oblong 6-inch leaflets.

Skimmia japonica. Slow growing to 2 to 5 feet, 3 feet or more wide. Clusters of very tiny white flowers held above the foliage in April and May. Both male and female plants necessary for berry production. Fruit: brilliant red holly-like berry in fall through December. Hardy to about 0°.

Ternstroemia gymnanthera (formerly called *T. japonica*). Slow growing to 4 to 6 feet high and as wide, smaller in containers. Can be held back by pruning. Handsome, dark green to bronze foliage, shiny in full sun. Cream colored, slightly fragrant ¾-inch flowers in May and June. Hardy to about 15°.

TREES FOR CONTAINERS

Golden wattle *(Acacia longifolia)*. Large billowy mass of dark green, evergreen foliage. Rapid growth to 15 feet and about as wide. Golden flowers in summer. Grows more compact in containers if shaped annually. Hardy to about 20°.

Other acacias suitable for containers are *A. pendula, A. retinodes,* and *A. verticillata.*

Japanese maple *(Acer palmatum)*. Slow growing to 12 feet. Many stemmed plant with small leaves deeply cut and saw-toothed. All year interest: young spring growth is glowing red; summer leaves are soft green; foliage turns scarlet in fall; slender leafless branches in greens and reds provide winter pattern. Hardy to 0°. Needs extra protection from sun and dry wind in hot interior climates. Two varieties are: Red Japanese maple *(A. p. atropurpureum)* with bronze, bronzy green, and green leaves, laceleaf Japanese maple *(A. p. dissectum)* with deeply dissected fern-like leaves.

Loquat *(Eriobotrya japonica)*. Small round-headed tree of moderate growth to 10 to 15 feet and about 15 feet wide. Bold, leathery, dark green leaves. Edible orange fruits. Good patio tree. Hardy to 20°.

Indian laurel fig *(Ficus retusa)*. Fast growing tree to 20 feet with somewhat pendulous growth habit. Dense dark green, glossy foliage. Grows well in restricted root area. Stands smoke, dust. Hardy to 25°.

Maidenhair tree *(Ginkgo biloba)*. Hardy deciduous tree to 70 to 80 feet in the ground, smaller and easily restricted in containers. Open, sparse, airy, sometimes gawky in youth, but always a picturesque character as it matures. Leathery leaves are light green in spring and summer, turning golden buttery-yellow in fall. Always buy cutting grown or grafted trees to be assured of getting male plants. (The female tree produces a flesh-covered nut that has an unpleasant odor.)

Grecian laurel, sweet bay *(Laurus nobilis)*. Slow growing tree to 6 to 8 feet in a container, normally compact with broad base gradually tapering to a cone; often with several trunks from the base. Dark green, ever-green foliage. Hardy to 20°, can be grown in colder climates if protected.

Japanese privet *(Ligustrum japonicum)*. Shrub or small round headed tree 10 to 12 feet high. Glossy medium green foliage. White flowers in clusters in late spring and summer with an odd, sometimes objectionable odor. Hardy to 15°.

Glossy privet *(Ligustrum lucidum)*. Small tree to 8 to 10 feet in containers. Deep green foliage. Creamy white flowers in late spring and summer with an odd odor. Hardy to 15°.

Evergreen magnolia *(M. grandiflora)*. Round headed tree, slow growing to 20 feet with a 15-foot spread in containers. Hardy to 15°. Dark green glossy leaves, brownish on the undersides. Large, white, fragrant flowers in summer. The new lower growing forms should be of especial interest to the container gardener.

Olive *(Olea europaea)*. Slow growing, round headed, bushy tree 10 to 15 feet tall with gray-barked branches. Older trees often have gnarled and twisted trunk. Gray-green, willow-like leaves. Black fruits in fall, which do drop as they ripen, unless picked. Hardy to 10°.

Palms. A number of small palms make ideal container plants. The pigmy date palm *(Phoenix loureiri)* is slow growing to 4 to 8 feet with 3 to 6-foot spread. Graceful with short slender trunk; lacy, arching fronds. Hardy to 18°. Paradise palm *(Howea forsteriana)* has upright to horizontal dark green fronds. Hardy to 28°. Lady Palm *(Raphis excelsa)*, a slow growing palm 5 to 12 feet tall with 3 to 7-foot spread. Shrubby clumps of straight bamboo-like stems bear a fibrous network of leaf sheaths. Hardy to 25°.

Mugho pine *(Pinus mugo mughus)*. Shrubby symmetrical plant usually no higher than 4 feet although it may become very spreading. Good dark green foliage. To keep small, pinch back new, soft green shoots about an inch in spring. Hardy.

Shore pine *(Pinus contorta)*. Very symmetrical, narrow-crowned tree when young; slender pyramidal crown when mature to 50 feet. Stands dwarfing well. Hardy.

Japanese black pine *(Pinus thunbergii)*. Slow growing tree, reaching 4 feet in about 3 to 4 years. Much used by Japanese in dwarf-tree training. Hardy.

LEFT. *Small redwood box, 10½ inches square, deeply scored, adds interest beside step. Mugho pine will stay small with roots confined, tips pinched back annually.*

CENTER. *Japanese black pine in octagonal 12-inch redwood tub.* RIGHT. *In a dramatic setting, a miniature conifer is an ever-changing form.*

Lath shelter was built to protect and display bonsai collection. Here is view toward house and added overhead that extends from living-dining area. Clump of camphor trees has developed well since planting eight years ago. Interesting variety of containers on shelf between posts is the result of patient shopping in old Japanese nurseries and pottery stores. Note that post construction gives structure a light, airy feeling. Four 8 by 2 by 2's are bolted to 3 by 6's and 2 by 4's overhead.

BONSAI: A SIMPLIFIED VERSION OF AN AGE-OLD ART

Bonsai, the Japanese art of growing living dwarfed trees in small containers, is a fairly painstaking technique, but it is still within the capabilities of many gardeners.

Here we tell how to select plants for bonsai training and how to plant, shape, and maintain them. The project will probably appeal to you most if you don't mind giving the plants constant care, and if your garden has reached the stage where it modifies extremes in heat, wind, and dryness. (Bonsai grow best outdoors in an almost perfect lathhouse type of environment.)

WHERE TO GET THE PLANTS

The best place for a gardener to seek bonsai plants is among the accidentally broken, untrained, or rootbound stock in nurseries. Look for interestingly misshapen plants—those with low horizontal growth, thick gnarled stems, and stocky branches. Fortunately, such plants are not hard to find. Ask the nurseryman to show you any stunted or misshapen plants he might have.

Since a bonsai should give the illusion of age—with trunk, branches, leaves, and flowers all miniature in scale —it's best to use only varieties that have relatively small flowers and foliage.

Start with as old a plant as possible. Cuttings of plants less than 5 years old do not offer much to work with; plants over 10 years of age are more valuable and interesting. Some plants grown from seed and cuttings are preferred because they look more natural. However, you could use a grafted plant in which the union is nearly invisible.

Now 15 years old, this deodar cedar was bought as a 4-year-old; repotted the following year with heavy root and top pruning; and repotted again two years later.

This Japanese black pine was transferred from a 5-gallon can 13 years ago. Has been in the present box for 10 years. Box is 18 inches square and 10 inches deep.

USE THE RIGHT CONTAINER

Because good bonsai pots are expensive, you, as a beginner, might prefer to use some of the inexpensive dishes made by ceramists or the shallow clay pots called fern pans. The container should be barely large enough to hold the plant.

PLANT IN SUFFICIENT SOIL

Start the bonsai in fall and winter when vegetative growth is slow. At that time you can handle plants with less danger of injuring growth, and flowering plants will establish in time for spring bloom.

Carefully wash soil from the plant's roots whether it is field or container soil. Do this work quickly in a cool, shaded location away from drying wind and sun. Roots will remain alive as long as a thin film or moisture covers them to exclude air. Therefore, keep them in water, thin mud, or damp moss as much as possible while you work.

As soon as you have exposed the roots, fit them into their new container. Usually you will have to prune them to make them fit, sometimes removing as much as half.

Unlike plants grown in ordinary containers or in the ground, a bonsai requires a rather heavy, water-retentive loam soil. Use leaf mold and peat moss sparingly, if at all, because these spongy materials tend to make soil in the tiny pots too loose and difficult to keep wet. Rich garden loam, to which about 10 per cent sharp sand and 10 per cent peat moss or well rotted leaf mold has been added, is a good basic mixture. The soil should be slightly damp and granular in texture, neither too fine nor too coarse.

Spread a thin layer of soil over the bottom of the container. Place the bare-root plant in the pot. Center it or put it at one end, and set it upright or at an angle. At all times work toward the final effect you desire. If you want, you can set the plant rather high to expose the crown and to show the tops of a few heavy roots; this helps to create the illusion of great size and age.

When you have the plant placed the way you want it, slowly add more soil around the roots and press it in firmly, filling every corner of the pot to a uniform hardness. Press in soil evenly so that the plant will stand firm and water will permeate every part of the container.

ELEMENTARY BONSAI. *1. When you shop for shrub to train, look for irregular horizontal growth.*

2. Wash dirt from roots in a pail or bucket of water. Be sure to keep the roots moist at all times as you work.

GROW IN PLEASANT SURROUNDINGS

Put a newly planted bonsai in a lathhouse, shaded patio, or sheltered corner of the garden, out of the bright sun, wind, and extreme cold. Water gently with a watering can or fine sprinkler spray until the water runs freely from the drainage hole. To prevent excessive evaporation, you can plunge the pot in a bed of wood shavings or peat moss, or tie a strip of burlap over the soil to shade the roots and keep the soil moist.

The critical factor in handling a new bonsai lies in keeping the soil and air around the plants evenly humidified. A fine mist sprayed over the plants once or twice a day is very beneficial.

In spring when roots become active again and top growth starts, you can handle your bonsai a bit more freely. But never expose it to full sun and wind because dryness is impossible to cope with in these tiny pots. Don't keep a bonsai in a greenhouse or in the house, either, for the greenhouse would force growth unnecessarily and the house would provide too little light and humidity. Best permanent exposure for a bonsai is the shelter of trees, lath, or protecting walls. It should have plenty of broken sunlight and be in a location accessible to water.

WATERING AND FEEDING

You must not water bonsai constantly because saturated soil is as dangerous as dry soil. But whenever the soil is dry, water it, even if this is necessary twice a day. Don't confuse spraying foliage with watering; the latter always must thoroughly soak the root ball. Bonsai is not for the gardener with little time. If the plant goes one day without water, years of work are cancelled.

Feed a bonsai sparingly, and only after it is well established. It can go a year without a feeding, and often is better for it. Excessive feeding forces too vigorous growth, out of keeping with the miniature scale of bonsai. And too much fertilizer may build up a harmful residue in the restricted soil area and burn the roots.

The best way of giving a bonsai more food is to repot it. If the plant shows poor leaf color or dries out too rapidly because of excessive rooting repot it in the same container or one slightly larger. Simply knock it from its pot while it is dormant. With a pointed stick, gently pick away one-fourth to half of the old soil, taking care not to damage the roots. Reset in fresh soil.

3. Choose containers according to root size and shape of plant. Pots in middle are domestic; others, Japanese.

4. If the container is small, prune the roots to make them fit. Note amount of material pruned off plant above. 5. To keep soil from washing out through the

bottom, place a piece of broken pot or small stone over hole. 6. Before you plant, try the plant in the container to decide if you want a horizontal or a vertical effect.

If it seems inconvenient or too soon to repot, feed the bonsai very sparingly with an organic fertilizer. Use liquid fish or animal manures at one-fourth the recommended strength two or three times in the fall or spring at six-week intervals. The purpose of the feeding is to give good color to the foliage and to maintain even growth—but not to force in any way. Thoroughly moisten soil in the pot before feeding.

HOW TO TRIM AND TRAIN TOP GROWTH

You can give the plants some preliminary pruning when you first pot them. Cut any twigs and branches which conflict with the form you have visualized. This helps

to balance the loss of roots that is often severe when you fit the plant to the container. Wait until the plants are thoroughly established again before you shape them in earnest.

Trimming, in bonsai culture, aims not so much at achieving symmetry as the rarer beauty of balance in assymetry. This doesn't mean that you should force the plants into strange and unnatural shapes. Work toward a picturesque naturalness, such as you encounter everywhere in nature.

Few plants will be so well shaped that they will make good bonsai subjects without trimming and dwarfing. But if you remember these two cardinal rules of the art, you cannot go far wrong: First, don't leave abrupt cuts

8. Once you have planted the bonsai, water gently until all the soil is saturated. Never permit roots to dry out. 9. Trim excess branches on newly potted plants,

but wait until plant is established before drastically shaping. 10. When you wire be sure not to injure the wood. You'll find branches pliable in active growth.

APLIN-DUDLEY STUDIOS

11. Each turn of wire should be one-half to one inch apart. Don't let the wire interfere with leaves or twigs.

12. To shape wired branches, hold in hands and gently bend into desired form. Bend wood cautiously.

where the top of the trunk or branches are lopped off. Second, don't bend or twist the stem or branches unnaturally.

The usual way to bend a stem or branch is to wind a wire around it in a spiral fashion. The weight of the wire, whether copper or galvanized, will vary with the caliper of the branch, but the wire must be strong enough to hold the bend in place. Do the wiring while the plants are in active growth as the wood is more pliable.

Twist the wire on the branches in spirals between one-half and one inch apart, beginning several inches below the bend and continuing to several inches beyond the first spiral. Avoid crushing or stripping the bark. Hold the wired branch with both hands and gently force it into the desired position. The tension of the wire spiral will hold it in place. In about a year, or before it girdles the branch, take the wire off, for the branch will be permanently bent by then.

This essential style of shaping a bonsai clearly articulates trunk and branches. Remove excess twigs and branches to allow the main lines of the plant to stand out. Sometimes you can shape twigs and branches by these methods: pinching the tips of the new growth in the spring and summer, spiral wiring or tying them to another branch, or cutting them rather drastically. Always keep the ideal form in mind, and once you achieve it, try to preserve it unchanged through the years.

Since the bonsai seeks to imitate the timelessness and grandeur of nature, you can plant the surface of its pot with a few stones and clumps of growing moss to enhance the illusion. In winter, a flowering bonsai will bloom with profusion; in spring it is clothed with delicate green; and in fall it ripens seed as though it were 10

feet instead of only 1 foot high. It is a conversation piece that can spend a day indoors and then go back to the garden again to grow and bloom.

CARE OF ESTABLISHED BONSAI

In recent years, the number of established bonsai displayed and sold in specialty nurseries has increased. These trees, ranging in age from 5 to 45 or 50 years, have been given constant care and patient training. Each is an original—it cannot be duplicated.

Bonsai plants cost from $10 to $15 for young trees and $20 to $75 and more for older ones. Because of the investment alone, a bonsai deserves more tender and loving care than you give the average potted plant. In fact, these miniature trees in containers require daily care to grow constantly, but not vigorously, as a bonsai plant should.

Here are some general rules on care and maintaining the trees shown here, from examples of typical imports.

Zelkova

Repotting. Once a year when the tree is dormant, repot zelkova to keep it from getting too tightly rootbound. After knocking the plant from the pot, use a pointed tool, small trowel, or chopstick, to knock off about one-third of the soil ball. Prune out old roots (those within the ball that are quite dark colored); leave the new lighter colored ones that are growing.

Use a soil mix containing approximately 60 per cent loam, 30 per cent sand, and 10 per cent humus (leaf mold or peat moss). Run this mixture through a 1/4-inch mesh screen to remove any large stones, sticks, or clods of soil and to produce a loose, granular mix.

ROOT PRUNING. 1. *Juniper, grown for 2 years in container, is ready for root pruning. Cut along edges to separate roots that adhere to container's inside surface.*

2. *Remove plant from its container by rocking root ball to free bottom roots. Place in tub of water, wash and work dirt off. Keep immersed, away from air.*

3. *Let plant soak in water one hour. Prepare container for replanting. Put broken pieces of flower pot over drainage holes; cover bottom surface with some gravel.*

4. *Next comes the root pruning. While helper holds tree, trim roots. When the job is finished, the root ball should be about half the width and depth you see here.*

5. *While the root-pruned plant is held at the position decided upon, helper carefully fills in with soil around the roots. Leave a few roots showing around the stem.*

6. *Now comes what many regard as the most fun: pruning the tree. Compare this picture with picture 1 on this page. You'll see that most of the cuts were small*

Left to right: Lebanon cedar, 5 years old; lodgepole pine, salal, 14; Japanese pine, 7; variegated juniper, 5; Indian cedar, 5; Himalayan pine, 21; Japanese pine, 7.

Zelkova is one of the easiest of deciduous trees for beginners in bonsai to grow. This one is 16 years old, and it is only 15 inches high. Should be repotted annually.

Satsuka azalea, estimated to be about 50 years old, measures 8 inches in height. Covered with white flowers in spring. Azaleas need replanting every 2 years.

Put the tree back in the same container from which it was taken. (It can grow in this container for many years if the roots are pruned and new soil is added each year.) Then work the soil in around the roots with a pencil or pointed stick, making sure there are no large air spaces. Plant moss on top of soil to help retain moisture and to reduce surface drying.

Watering. Water zelkova whenever the surface of the soil becomes dry. In most cases this means daily watering. Where the air is very warm and dry, you may have to water as much as twice daily. Use a fine spray nozzle or sprinkling can to water plants. To avoid leaf burn, don't wet foliage of broad leafed deciduous trees at midday.

You may find that a large number of plants in small containers can be more easily and thoroughly watered if set in a pan of water to absorb moisture from beneath. Don't let them soak too long, however. Remove them from the pan as soon as water has traveled through the soil and wet the surface.

Pruning. In the spring when about six leaves have developed on the new growth, pinch back to three leaves. Throughout the summer keep new growth pinched back to maintain the existing design of the plant.

Azalea

The azalea—one of the easiest plants to cultivate as a bonsai—is highly recommended for the beginner.

BLAIR STAPP

Juniper, originally transplanted from high mountain elevations to be trained as bonsai. Age: 45 to 50 years. Height: 21 inches. They need repotting every 4 years.

Handsome Japanese black pine (Pinus thunbergii) is about 75 years old, but stands only 18 inches high. Has rugged appearance of grown tree exposed to elements.

Repotting. Azaleas need not be transplanted more often than once every two years. Repot them during the winter months when the shrub is dormant. Follow the directions given for zelkova.

Watering. Don't let the soil dry out too much. Azaleas like a moist soil. If growth becomes too rank, reduce moisture slightly. They also like to have water sprayed on their leaves early in the day, but don't wet the plants when in flower. Water will spot the blooms.

Pruning. After bloom in spring, azaleas develop two large leaves and a small one and one or more shoots. Pinch out these shoots as they develop.

Cotoneaster

Repotting. Flower and fruit bearing shrubs need repotting each year. Transplant cotoneaster immediately after flowering in spring. Cut back roots every 2 years as described for zelkova. Use a loose, porous potting soil containing about 40 per cent sand, 50 per cent loam, and 10 per cent peat moss and leaf mold.

Watering. Rules for watering are those described for zelkova.

Pruning. Since cotoneasters are very fast growers, they require regular pruning from the time flowers drop in spring, until August. Keep new growth pinched back and one or more shoots at ends of the branches. Pinch out these shoots.

Pines

Repotting. Use 40 per cent sand, 50 per cent loam, and 10 per cent screened humus for a potting soil. Pea gravel in the bottom of the pot insures the good drainage pines need. When you repot a plant, prune out older roots in the way prescribed for zelkova. Repot pines no more than once every three or four years.

Watering. Water pines at least once a day to provide adequate moisture. Although they don't require as much water around their roots as deciduous trees, the sandy soil dries out quickly. Pines like to have water sprayed over their needles once or twice a day. Use a fine mist spray in the morning and evening.

Pruning. To control both the growth of the tree and the size of the needles, pinch out new growth that appears in the spring. This encourages side shoots with small needles. Remove lower needles if they become too thick or too long.

Juniper, chamaecyparis

Repotting and watering procedures for junipers and chamaecyparis are similar to those for pines.

Pruning. Pinch out the new growth on junipers as it comes out in the spring. Chamaecyparis is constantly growing and requires frequent and regular pinching throughout the growing season. Remove tiny young tips to keep growth compact.

Conifers do well in the shallowest of containers and, therefore, permit planting of miniature landscapes. This is Colorado blue spruce (Picea pungens glauca), fitted into a ceramic container 3 inches deep, 7 inches wide, 11 long.

HOW TO GROW "ADAPTED" BONSAI

For the gardener who delights in dwarfed plants, but wishes they could be developed without the usual process of binding and twisting, "adapted bonsai" offers a happy substitute.

Roots of the plants shown here (also, top left, p. 76) have not been trimmed severely; their tops have not been wired or bent. Their only resemblance to true bonsai, other than their appearance, lies in the fact that they have been potted in small containers in which most of them will remain indefinitely. Confined root space keeps them small. They are fed only occasionally.

For adapted bonsai try to find seedling trees and shrubs in 2½-inch pots. If they are pot-bound, so much the better, since the root ball will remain intact when you shift it. Select the smallest size container that will accommodate the root ball.

Water the plant a day or two before repotting. If you are using a very small container, knock the plant out of the pot and press the root ball in your hands to compact soil as much as possible. Gently maneuver the root ball into the container, taking care not to injure or break roots. In some cases you may have to cut the taproots that are too long to fit into the container. The plants shown here are potted high, with the crown above the soil surface. You may place a small rock or clump of moss near the root crown to give it support as well as to complete the composition.

Although small conifers are ideal for adapted bonsai, you can also use slow growing, broad leafed evergreens such as rhododendrons, azaleas, and heathers; or deciduous trees such as Japanese maple, ginkgo, and dwarf apple and pear. Since all of these plants are hardy outdoors, they make ideal terrace subjects. Any stay indoors should be brief—and in a cool place. Keep the plants moist, particularly those in very small pots.

Shop with an eye for plant structure

Our garden editor went nursery shopping with a bonsai specialist. From the nursery rows, they chose five plants— probably the most "imperfect" in the nursery—that by their form suggested an interesting future. Photographs of three of them, as bought at the nursery and then as transferred to pots and lightly shaped, are shown on these pages.

To the bonsai grower, there are no abstract standards —a fir does not have to look like a specimen fir, a pine is not necessarily a model of a pine tree. The form of each plant he sees exists independently of all other plants.

Junipers

There is no question about the ability of the juniper to create interesting forms. But in selecting a single plant, it is wise to know the growing habits of the species and varieties if the plant is to be grown in a restricted space.

Self-rooted Meyer lemon is a vigorous grower but can be kept in small container by severe top and root-pruning for 2 to 3 years. Soil in pot is planted with ground cover (baby tears) mounded, and landscaped with rocks.

Low-growing, creeping forms of juniper do best in restricted space. The type of container you choose—round, square, oval—will depend upon how you picture the plant. This is a conventional Japanese bonsai pot. Note pebble mulch.

Better avoid the large, vigorous growers and make your selection within the naturally low growing forms. Look for specimens among the following: Creeping juniper—its varieties Bar Harbor and Andorra are two of the most interesting; tamarix juniper is normally low growing; Armstrong's juniper is widely available.

Meyer lemon

Unless you buy a Meyer lemon that has been grafted on dwarf rootstock, don't assume that you have a small shrub. Seedlings will often take off with very vigorous growth and reach a height of 6 feet or more. However, the Meyer lemon is amenable to both top and root pruning, and you can hold it to almost any size in a container. Fortunately, the Meyer lemon will bear fruit as both a

youthful and a small plant. It will live for several years in a 12 to 14-inch tub, but when grown in a very small container, it should be regarded as only a temporary 2 to 3-year affair.

Spruce

The number of nurseries carrying spruce trees dwindles as you move from the Northwest southward. If you plan on restricting root space in a container, almost any form will be satisfactory. However, there are three dwarf forms that naturally grow to no more than 3 feet in height—*Picea abies procumbens, P. a. nidiformis,* and *P. glauca conica.* The first two are rounded plants, while *P. glauca conica* is a slender miniature tree with a base spread of only 1 foot.

Colorado blue spruce *(Picea pungens glauca)* gets into a lot of trouble in localities with dry summers. Generally, the easiest conifers to grow when you follow bonsai culture are the pines, junipers, and deodar cedar. These plants do not suffer from being held in a can in a nursery and maintain their good looks under the most adverse conditions.

Strawberry guava

Strawberry guava *(Psidium cattleianum),* in its normal growth where winter temperatures stay above 25°, becomes a large evergreen shrub to 18 to 20 feet. There is great variation in growth habit, but most of those you find in the nurseries are less sparse than the one shown here. Pruning both top and root will keep it at almost any size desired.

Normally in August and September, this plant bears many claret-red edible fruits 1½ inches wide. Although the strawberry guava will bear as a very small shrub, such severe leaf removal as done here will prevent fruit development.

Indoor foliage plants become part of architectural scheme in contemporary houses with flow of space between outdoors and interior. Here, philodendron on the wall and tubbed philodendron and monstera near window, bring garden indoors and blend with natural construction materials — brick, rough-sawn roof.

80 HOUSE PLANTS

HOUSE PLANTS: EASY ENOUGH TO GROW IF YOU PROVIDE THE RIGHT ENVIRONMENT

A revolution in indoor gardening has occurred within the last 10 or 15 years. In that time we have changed over almost completely from gardening indoors to indoor designing with plants.

This change is linked directly to a change in house design—from small windows to large expanses and even walls of glass. But more important has been our discovery that plants are structural forms with a design value demonstrated by the architect and interior designer.

We no longer think of indoor plants only as colorful or beautiful individuals. We appraise them for their form and texture. We use them in "well balanced compositions." They are "bold" and "cast dramatic shadows" or "repeat outdoor forms."

Demonstrations have not been limited to the modern glass house. The dish garden, the portable planter, and all the various containers of the florist shop and the nursery furnish backgrounds for designs with foliage plants.

The indoor gardener interested primarily in color or just the pleasure of watching plants grow has lost nothing by the increased interest in foliage plants. Because of the increasing demand, suppliers have made available a wider selection of all types of indoor plants. The illustrations in this chapter show the wide variety in plant structural form.

APLIN-DUDLEY STUDIOS

Built-in planter with dracaena, philodendron, ivy is lined with metal, has water-tight drawer to catch seepage. Could also be filled with peat, plants in pots.

MAYNARD L. PARKER

Planting bed sunk in floor provides ample growing space for indoor plants, requires cultural techniques similar to those for large container. Bed divides room.

Garden inside the house. Glass wall provides light needed by growing plants and a wide view from both garden area and upstairs living room.

Foliage plants grow in planting pocket which juts out into glass walled bay and brings garden into house. Open plan gives pleasant, airy feeling of summer house.

CHECKLIST OF INDOOR FOLIAGE PLANTS

The homeowner who is interested in displaying foliage plants indoors will find a wide choice before him in the nurseries. However, not all of the plants on sale are easy to grow. Following is a selection of the most trouble-free of these decorative plants:

Aglaonema robelinii (rear). Robust grower; thick stems; wide, leathery, 10-inch leaves mottled with gray. *A. commutatum* (front) has narrow 6-inch leaves with silver markings. Both thrive in poor light and need rich fibrous loam. They are good in dish gardens or on a mantel.

Taller is **Sansevieria trifasciata laurentii.** Slow growing. Erect, thick, 2½-foot, spear-like leaves, light green marked with gray when young, becoming dark green striped with golden yellow. Other is *S. hahnii,* low growing, compact clumps of dark green leaves mottled gray when young. Both take any exposure, dark or light, any soil, cold to warm temperatures. Water them well but infrequently.

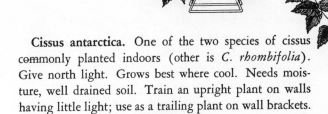

Cissus antarctica. One of the two species of cissus commonly planted indoors (other is *C. rhombifolia*). Give north light. Grows best where cool. Needs moisture, well drained soil. Train an upright plant on walls having little light; use as a trailing plant on wall brackets.

Miniature date palms *(Phoenix loureiri)* planted with acuba and fern. Likes filtered sun or north light, cool or warm temperature, heavy soil, constant moisture, prefers being root-bound. Use in dish gardens, single plant in bronze container, in window box with similar plants.

Tolmiea menziesii. Grows to 2 feet. Heart-shaped, fresh green leaves produce new plantlets at tips of leaf stalks. Takes all exposures. Needs moisture, light soil. It is a very rugged house plant. Use in dish gardens with other hardy plants, or as specimen on window sills or tables.

Dieffenbachia amoena (dark). Broad, leathery, dark green leaves with white slanting stripes on either side of midrib. Suitable for large room where 2-foot plant would be in scale. *D. picta* Rudolph Roehrs. Chartreuse green leaves blotched ivory and edged in green. Showy as single plant, in green-toned rooms, against dark woodwork. Dieffenbachia likes north light and high temperatures. Give water sparingly.

Philodendron radiatum. Slow growing climber. Dark green, arrow-shaped, 9-inch leaves irregularly divided by deep cuts on either side of midrib. Good for small places where unusual leaf and slow growth desired. Full north light or indirect sun. Even temperature, does best at about 60°.

Philodendron sodiroi (taller). Heart-shaped leaves mottled with silver gray. Most attractive when small; keep in small container. *Maranta leuconeura kerchoveana.* Spreading, to 1 foot. Light green, roundish, 7-inch leaves with chocolate brown spots when young; turning to rich velvety emerald green. Likes north light, light soil, good drainage, temperatures to 60° or above, abundant water.

CARE OF INDOOR PLANTS

Indoor plants are much more dependent on the care and consideration of the gardener than are those grown in the garden. A shrub or tree in the open ground usually manages to shift for itself through a period of neglect that would kill an ordinary house plant.

When you make an indoor planting, remember that in most cases you are transferring plants from the environment of a greenhouse especially planned for their health to rooms planned not for plants to thrive in, but for man's comfort.

Rather than attempt to approach greenhouse conditions or humidity in the living room, the successful indoor gardener tries to reduce the hazard of the unnatural environment by using special care in watering, drainage, and feeding.

Water and drainage

Correct watering is the most important requirement in the care of indoor plants. House plants will tolerate neither sogginess about the roots nor drying out.

When to water varies with several factors, including the nature of the plant, humidity, the amount of natural light (which regulates transpiration), temperature, size of root system, and soil structure.

However, as plants are inarticulate, there remains only one way to judge their watering needs—and that is by testing the soil below the surface. If it is no longer moist, it is time to water.

Dish and tray gardens. In the greenhouse, all foliage plants are grown in containers with drainage holes in the bottom. Watering is part of a regular schedule. However, when the plants are taken into the house, watertight containers such as bowls and trays are often used.

Therefore, an entirely different set of rules for watering and drainage must be followed.

Some allowance is made for lack of drainage in dish gardens by using a thin layer of charcoal on the bottom to prevent souring, and a layer of peat moss or vermiculite above that to absorb water. Even with these materials present, indiscriminate day-to-day watering will cause sogginess, because the containers will hold all the water that the peat or vermiculite cannot absorb after being saturated.

Due to the varied conditions of heat, light, and humidity in the home, you cannot set aside certain days of the week for watering dish gardens. Instead, test the soil with the finger tips 3 or 4 times weekly, and water only when the soil underneath is no longer damp.

Drained containers. Where drainage is provided in the container—such as clay pots and plant boxes—treat the bottom of the container as follows:

Place pieces of broken crockery over the holes to prevent clogging by the soil. A layer of pebbles is sometimes placed over the crockery. Over that put a layer of coarse material such as sphagnum moss, which acts as a sieve to prevent soil above from washing through.

Soil

It is not advisable to use finely sifted soil in preparing the potting mixture. Most soils, when sifted through a fine screen, pack down to a hard cake after the first watering. Use a coarse screen to sift out only large rocks and debris. At the Golden Gate Park Conservatory in San Francisco, soil for potting tropical plants in large containers is never sifted. Experience there has proved that coarser soil particles, rocks, and decayed vegetable matter in unsifted soil keeps the soil loose and benefits drainage.

MINIATURE FOLIAGE PLANTS. LEFT. *Put dry mix in dish and compose planting while plants are in pots. Here a* nephthytis Silver Queen *is worked down to fit.*

CENTER. *Scooped-out place ready for roots. See how much dirt rubbed off roots.* **RIGHT.** *Little plants thrive in containers. Water with plastic clothes sprinkler.*

BLAIR STAPP

How to revive a tired planter: LEFT. *This old planter has lost its lushness; the plants are too leggy and sparse to be on display. Hard water has left a whitish deposit caked on the soil (in soft-water areas the surface might be mossy).* CENTER. *Best to dump it out and start all over again with new soil, new plants. Clean and polish the container.* RIGHT. *New soil and new plants rejuvenate planter for another 3 months. Tall plant in center is* Dieffenbachia *Julius Roehrs. Two variegated peperomias occupy left end,* Philodendron oxycardium *base.*

Equally helpful in drainage is rough leaf mold. One large-scale grower uses a potting mixture of 3 parts loam to 1 part rough leaf mold, with a handful of bone meal worked in for each pot.

Several good ready-made plant mixes are available on the markets.

Large-scale planting

In large architecturally designed plant boxes, potted plants are often plunged, pot and all, into peat moss or sphagnum rather than planted directly in the large container. This way watering can be more easily controlled and plants readily replaced.

Light

A position near a north window furnishes just the right amount of diffused natural light for plants native to shaded jungles, as are most house plants.

Very few foliage plants can tolerate direct sunlight, especially when it is magnified through clear glass. For that reason, avoid placing them directly behind or below windows which face the midday sun.

Variegated foliage plants always need more light than do solid green varieties. Leaf cells in the white spots contain little or no chlorophyll and hence are not capable of carrying on photosynthesis or food manufacturing. When a variegated plant is placed in a dark corner, the few green cells present in the leaves cannot manufacture enough carbohydrates to maintain a healthy growing condition.

Many gardeners move their house plants onto a shaded terrace or lanai for the summer months. However, sudden changes of temperature can be damaging; do not move house plants outside when there is much difference between inside and outside temperatures. For the same reason, they should not be taken out into the rain. It is better to keep a reserve supply of rain water on hand for watering.

Heat and humidity

The hot air given off by a modern heating apparatus is quite dry. This excessive aridity is fatal to plants which thrive in humid conditions. Temperatures in the high 70's will kill plants more sensitive to dry air unless the heat is supplemented by some sort of humidifier, as a wet sponge at the heat source. Many foliage plants thrive in the bathroom because of the humidity from bathing and showering.

Temperatures can drop as low as 40° without much ill effect on most house plants. Unheated bedrooms with moist air are ideal for many foliage plants.

Give your plants plenty of fresh air and ventilation, but avoid cold drafts.

Nourishment

As a rule, a sickly looking plant isn't necessarily in need of plant food. Pests or faulty soil or drainage conditions may cause the trouble. Here, again, learning to understand your potted plants will help you in planning a feeding schedule.

If the original potting mixture is rich in nutrients, the plant won't need any fertilizer until the roots have

GARDEN IN A SNIFTER. *This kind of planter goes for months with water you give it at planting time.* LEFT. *Fill ¼ full with dry vermiculite.* CENTER. *Place largest plant first. Here a golden variegated croton*

goes in. Root ball was crumbled to fit. RIGHT. *Water when plants are set. Sprinkle until you see water on surface. That will be all for several months—gets humid in there. Snifters make bright, decorative display*

nearly filled the container. If the soil is sandy and weak in nutrients, plants may require a feeding shortly after planting. A feeding schedule depends, too, on the size of the container and the number and type of plants contained.

When you conclude that your plants are in need of fertilizer, it's best to use a water soluble dry fertilizer or a liquid commercial plant food.

Dust and insects

House dust is another foreign factor with which indoor plants must contend. Leaves covered with a film of dust cannot carry on transpiration in the normal manner. To

keep them free of dust, clean the leaves, top and bottom, with a damp cloth or sponge once or twice a month.

Routine washing will also keep the plants clean of insects. However, hard water will spot the leaves. Thrips, red spider and mealy bugs are particularly bad on some house plants. You can buy pressurized aerosol cans with insecticides specially formulated for indoor plants.

HOW TO PROPAGATE HOUSE PLANTS

Early summer is a good time to reshape or propagate house plants. After spending a winter indoors, plants may be leggy and in need of pinching and cutting back. From the pieces you cut off, you can easily grow new

Unusual plant container shown here was made from refrigeration insulation cork. Cut to size with band saw, then hollow out block with paring knife or jacknife. Because cork is porous, line container with plastic wood, which also has rough finish. Tint plastic wood, if you like, to combine or contrast with rough dark brown cork. Philodendron and sansevieria are planted in finished container shown at the right.

Sampling of clean-line planters available for house plants. Dish on tray in foreground has drain holes— plants in it will live longer than in no-hole dishes.

plants to replenish your supply; or share the cuttings with friends.

The only equipment you need is a box filled with sand, sand and peat moss, or straight pumice, perlite, or vermiculite. Cover the box with a piece of glass or inexpensive plastic screening, and you're in business.

There are actually five ways in which you can propagate house plants vegetatively: by leaf cuttings, stem cuttings, softwood cuttings, mallet cuttings, and layering.

Leaf cuttings

Probably the easiest method of increasing indoor foliage plants is by leaf cuttings. African violet, peperomia, and sansevieria can be propagated in this way.

The leaf—or, in the case of sansevieria, a portion of it—will root easily in clean, sharp river sand. Firm the

cuttings in the rooting medium, and keep it moist but not wet until cuttings are rooted and ready to transplant into the potting medium.

Softwood cuttings

Philodendron, ivy, and croton are readily propagated from softwood cuttings. From the stem, take a cutting

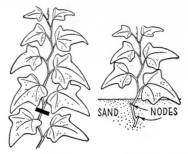

2 to 3 inches in length with 2 to 3 sets of leaves attached. With a sharp knife, cut the stem from the parent plant just below a leaf node. Remove foliage from the lower portion which will be below the surface of the rooting medium. Dip the cut end into hormone powder to hasten rooting. Then plant the cuttings, firm the medium, and water thoroughly to establish contact between the cutting and the rooting medium. Roots will develop at the base of the cutting and around the leaf nodes or joints.

Mallet cuttings

Rubber plant, and many of the philodendrons with wide-spaced leaves, can be propagated by mallet cuttings. A mallet cutting is a stem section with a leaf attached to it. It resembles a mallet, with the stem section as the head and the leaf as the handle.

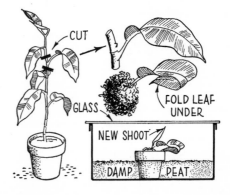

Wrap this type of cutting with moist moss up to the base of the leaf petiole, or root it in any of the other rooting mediums. A new shoot will sprout from the bud in the axil of the leaf.

HOUSE PLANTS **87**

Layering

Layering is a method of propagation frequently used on many of the philodendrons and ivies with vining growth habit.

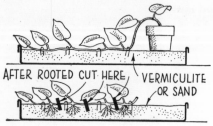

AFTER ROOTED CUT HERE VERMICULITE OR SAND

Bend the stems over and lay them in a horizontal position on the rooting medium. Peg the stems securely to the medium. After roots have formed, cut the stem into sections. The roots formed at each node will be the start of a new plant.

AIR-LAYERING . . . STEP BY STEP

The art of air-layering, practiced by Chinese horticulturists thousands of years ago, is undergoing something of a revival. With the recent introduction of improved materials for retaining moisture, air-layering promises to become an important method for propagating plants that are difficult to root from cuttings, and for tall and lanky, one-stemmed plants that cannot be bent to the ground for tip-layering or which offer no side shoots for cutting material.

The principle behind this method is really quite simple. The stem is cut, girdled, or scarified to stimulate root formation. When the roots have formed, they and the section of the stem above are cut off and become a separate plant.

Here we show in eight steps how to air-layer a dieffenbachia. You can use the same method on any plant suitable for air-layering—or as a more foolproof method of growing many cutting-propagated plants.

The best time for air-layering, the ideal stem diameter, and the proper degree of maturity vary with the plant and species. Gardeners generally learn through trial and error.

An important factor in successful air-layering is keeping the moss constantly wet around the cut in the stem. Clay pots (hinged, slit, or cut in half for the purpose), composition pots, and heavy waxed paper have all been used with some degree of success. However, the best material of all for holding moisture in the moss around

BEFORE. *To make this tall gangling* Dieffenbachia bausei *a low, showy plant again, you can air-layer it as shown in the photos that follow—not too difficult.*

AFTER. *Here is the Dieffenbachia about 2 months after being air-layered. Photo shows newly rooted upper portion after it was potted, as shown at the right.*

the cut is a plastic product known as polyethylene film, which retains moisture yet permits gases to escape.

This film can be wrapped around the sphagnum ball and fastened with string, plant ties, or a tape resistant to water, oil, and acid. Method of wrapping with polyethylene film is shown at the right. Overlap the film on the underside of the branch and carefully fasten it to the branch at top and bottom of the ball to prevent excess

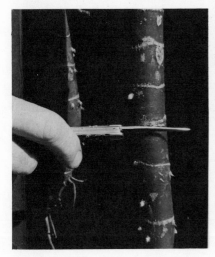

1. Cut into stem below node (see position of blade). Note nubbins along stem where new roots originate.

2. Cut ½ to ⅔ of the way through stem, bracing back of cane with splint so it will not snap off at the cut.

3. Take a couple handfuls of moist sphagnum moss. Place small amount in cut, rest around wound. Tie.

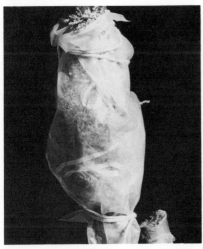

4. To keep sphagnum moist, wrap plastic film all the way around ball, tying it in place at top and bottom.

5. When roots form above cut portion of stem and show through wrap, sever rooted portion from parent.

6. Removing top from parent plant forces growth of lateral bud, which in time produces a new top, as shown.

water from seeping under the film and causing rot.

Several companies now offer air-layering kits. Each kit includes sphagnum moss, rooting hormones, plant ties, and enough polyethylene film to make 8 to 10 layers. In some kits the plastic is coated with the rooting hormones and a fungicide so they can be rubbed over the cut rather than dusted on. *(Caution:* An excess amount of hormone will injure the tissues rather than induce quicker rooting.)

To purchasers of kits we offer this word of advice: Air-layering is not the quick, easy method of propagation that some manufacturers would like you to believe. Air moisture is all-important in successful air-layering, and almost impossible to maintain outdoors. Quickest and most certain results with air-layering are obtained in a greenhouse where proper humidity can be maintained at all times. The polyethylene film has points in its favor, but even with the aid of this material, air-layering is no foolproof propagation panacea.

A variety of plants have been successfully propagated by air-layering. They include such indoor foliage plants as cordyline, dieffenbachia, dracaena, ficus, and pandanus.

A duPont hybrid above, double-flowered hybrid below.

African violet duPont Blue hybrid in wood container.

AFRICAN VIOLETS: THE NUMBER-ONE FLOWERING HOUSE PLANT

The African violet undoubtedly holds claim to the number one position among indoor flowering plants. For a full discussion of the selection and care of this delightful plant, see the *Sunset* Book, *How to Grow African Violets* by Carolyn K. Rector.

Here are answers to the questions most frequently asked regarding culture of the African violet:

Should I water my plants from the top or the bottom? Either method is practical. When watering from the top, do so early in the morning. Avoid watering the leaves or into the crown of the plant.

Should I keep the plants wet or dry? Try to keep the soil between the two extremes. Water well, then do not water again until the surface of the soil feels slightly dry to the touch. Never let water stand in the pot saucer more than two hours after watering.

Should I use warm or cold water? Use tepid water or water at room temperature. If you accidentally splash it on the leaves, it won't make ring-shaped spots on them.

Do African violets require sun or shade? An east window with a roof overhang or suffused morning sun give the best light for a year-around location. Avoid south exposures and afternoon sun. A northern exposure is fine in summer but may be too dark during the winter.

What shall I feed my African violets, and how frequently should I feed them? Any liquid or water soluble commercial fertilizer which is slightly on the acid side is good. If the plant is well established, feed every two to four weeks during the growing season. Apply fertilizers only when the soil is moist. Follow the label directions.

What is the best temperature for African violets? African violets will grow well and bloom profusely at temperatures of 70° during the day, 60° or above at night.

What is the best potting mixture for violets? Four basic ingredients make a good soil mix for African violets: garden soil, a soil conditioner (sand, vermiculite, pumice, perlite), an acid humus (peat moss or leaf mold), and a slow acting fertilizer (manure, bone meal). One satisfactory mix consists of 3 parts leaf mold, 1 part loam, 1 part well rotted manure, and ½ part coarse sand.

In what medium should I plant violet leaves after rooting them in water? Sterilized sand, vermiculite, pumice, or perlite are the best mediums for potting newly rooted leaves. Later, move the young plants to the regular mix described above.

Repotting African violets

When your African violets become misshapen from a multiple growth of crowns, or when plants form trunks and literally grow out of the pot, it's time to divide and transplant them. After repotting, water plants thoroughly by plunging each pot to the rim in a pan of tepid water.

Step 1. To remove the plant from its container, cut around the edge with a knife, loosening soil and roots from wood. By slipping a small garden fork under the root ball, you can lift it out without breaking it. To remove plants from clay pots, gently tap sides and bottom, invert pot, and root ball should slip right out.

Step 2. Take out divisions. Hidden beneath the leaves are new plant crowns. If left, they will destroy the symmetrical rosette of foliage produced by a single crown. But if they are gently cut or broken from the

mother plant as shown above, and potted, they will develop into large blooming plants like the original one.

Step 3. Pot up divisions. Suggested mix for rooted plants: 1 part soil, 1 part leaf mold, 1 part sand and vermiculite or peat moss. Growers' mixers vary. Some use almost pure leaf mold.) Add ½ tablespoon superphosphate, 1 tablespoon bone meal (slowly available to plant). Grow crowns with few or no roots in sand, or ½ sand and ½ peat moss or vermiculite. When rooted, repot in a richer mixture.

Step 4. Place broken crock or charcoal in bottom of pot for drainage. Fill in around roots with potting soil. Keep crown of plant above soil surface. Firm soil with thumbs. For quicker rooting dip unrooted divisions in hormone powder before planting. If potted carefully, blooming plants will keep right on flowering after move.

A 3-foot pole encased in wire forms the frame for this column of African violets. For details, see sketch.

African violets climb a pole

Here is a novel way to display African violets and it doesn't require nearly as much space as a whole shelf-ful of pots. Plant the violets on a moss covered pole. A 3-foot pole will provide growing space for about 20 plants.

It will also facilitate your job of maintaining the high humidity, warmth, moisture, and rapid drainage essential to the good growth of African violets.

To make a pole 6 inches in diameter, you will need these: 4 pounds fresh green sphagnum moss, a 20 by 36-inch piece of plaster wire or chicken wire (or any firm wire with about 2-inch mesh), a 1 by 1-inch redwood stake 30 inches long, a round lid cut from a No. 2½ tin can, ½ pound of granulated or chicken charcoal, a small package of water-soluble house plant food, a 3-inch clay flower pot, and an 8 or 10-inch clay or ceramic pot.

To construct the pole, lay the wire out flat. Soak the sphagnum moss in a solution containing 1 teaspoon water-soluble fertilizer to 1 gallon of water. After it has been well drained, spread 3 inches of the sphagnum evenly over the wire. Sprinkle a layer of charcoal on the moss. Nail the lid to the bottom of the 1-inch redwood stake to balance it and keep the charcoal core from falling out. Lay the stake in the middle of the blanket of moss and charcoal keeping the lid flush with one end. Roll the moss and charcoal firmly around the stake overlapping the wire about 2 inches. (Unless the moss is

wrapped very firmly it will be impossible to keep it moist.) Tuck the ends of the wire under and fasten them securely.

Set the pole firmly in a large 8 or 10-inch pot, bracing it well with rocks, gravel, fir bark, burned shale, or any medium that will drain quickly. In the top of the pole, sink a 3-inch pot so that its top is level with the top of the pole. Fill the drainage hole in the bottom of the pot with a glass wick or a wad of nylon stocking so the water will drip slowly.

You will find that standard or semi-miniature varieties of African violets are best choices for pole culture; large foliaged varieties soon look too big for the pole and, when planted between smaller forms, quickly cover them up.

Before planting, carefully wash the soil off the violet roots and wrap them in a 1-inch ball of moist sphagnum. Make a hole in the moss pole large enough for the root ball. Press the plant firmly in place by sticking your finger in above the plant and pressing down on the root ball. This leaves a depression in the moss that can be used later to test for moisture inside the pole. Space the plants to avoid overlapping the leaves.

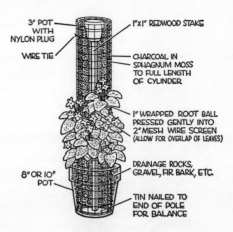

The inside of the pole pictured above looks like this. The redwood stake surrounded by charcoal forms the core. A large container supports the pole.

After planting, keep the moss continually moist by filling the pot at the top of the pole with warm water. Feed once a month in the same manner, using ¼ teaspoonful water soluble plant food to each quart of warm water. Check the plants at the bottom of the pole from time to time to be sure all are receiving equal moisture. Keep the pole in a warm, light location, but not in direct sunlight. Rotate it daily to keep the plants growing evenly around the pole.

*To dress up an indoor orchid display,
set pans in wrought iron stands,
pots in ceramic containers.*

ORCHIDS: NO LONGER JUST FOR EXPERTS

Orchids offer a challenge to the indoor gardener. Unlike philodendron, ivy, and a few other house plants that get along with minimum care, orchids need special treatment.

In general, the life cycle of all orchids is the same. Only the timing and details differ. They grow, they bloom, they go dormant, and they must have a specific kind of care at each stage. Consider the cultural requirements of the groups below, then choose the ones you feel will be easiest to handle in your situation.

Cattleya

This is the one most people think of when they hear the word "orchid." Commonest forms are purple, but there is a wide color range. The long pseudo-bulbs—the distinctive, thickened stem sections which provide

food and water storage for the plant—support the stiff, leathery leaves. Bloom time differs with kind, but by careful selection, you may get year-around bloom. They require: high light intensity (about 80 per cent of outdoor light intensity), high humidity (between 60 to 80 per cent), and a year-around temperature of 60° to 70°.

Cypripedium

Some forms of this lovely "ladyslipper" orchid grow wild in forests of the Pacific Northwest. The elegant flowers have such a high gloss that they look lacquered.

Most of the mottled-leaf forms will grow in a cool corner of the house; others, such as *C. insigne,* should have slightly cooler conditions. Most bloom in the late fall, winter, and early spring. Select kinds that extend the blooming period. They require: medium to low light

Cattleya   *Cypripedium*   *Dendrobium*   *Epidendrum*

intensity, high humidity, and a year-around temperature of 50° to 60°.

Keep moist at all times. In the home where humidity is at a minimum, place the potted orchid in a saucer of water and rewater whenever the saucer is empty.

Dendrobium

D. nobile, one of the most popular species in this group, has thin pseudo-bulbs nearly cylindrical in shape; grows to 2½ feet, with a woody, bamboo-like character. The flowers—2½ to 3 inches across—are borne in groups of 2 or 3. Petals are white at the base, with light amber tips and a dark eye. It blooms from January to June. This species is leafless during dormancy. The newer Hawaiian hybrids are now much more widely grown because they bloom over a longer period, are available in a wider color range, and are easier to grow.

Dendrobiums require high light intensity, high humidity, and a temperature of 70° or more from March until the terminal leaf on the new growth is fully mature —in September or October.

When foliage yellows, gradually withhold water, giving only enough to keep the pseudo-bulb from shriveling during the dormant period. Resume watering when buds swell in spring. Keep at a temperature of about 50° to 55° during dormancy.

Epidendrum

Although maybe not quite as rewarding to grow as some of the orchids, the epidendrums are probably the easiest and one of the faster growers. They are epiphytss with thickened reed-like stems. Clusters of miniature orchids, resembling in shape the cattleya flower, come in shades of yellow, orange, lavender, and rose depending on the species or variety.

Culture of this group of orchids is the same as for cattleyas. But unlike the cattleya, they will also grow in a good well drained soil mix. Fertilize the plants about once a month with orchid fertilizer. They make ideal patio container plants, too, since they can be grown outdoors in full sun during the summer months up until

the first frost—then placed in a protective patio or green-house.

Laelia

L. anceps, the species most generally grown by the amateur, looks in every way like a scaled-down cattleya orchid. Flowers in December and January—usually two or three to a stem—are generally rose purple. There are white forms, also.

Culture is similar to that for the cattleya. Plants require a definite rest period after flowering.

Oncidium

This epiphytic orchid is often known as the dancing lady, because of its long arching sprays of yellow and brown flowers that resemble a ballerina. Flowers come in fall and winter. Foliage is yellow green and borne at the top of a short oval pseudo-bulb.

Give oncidiums lots of light and good air circulation. They thrive in both cool and warm temperatures—50° to 65°.

Odontoglossum

Often known as the tiger orchid, *O. grande* produces large, showy, bright yellow flowers, striped with brown, in sprays about 1 foot long. Pseudo-bulbs, from 2 to 4 inches high, support thick, dull green leaves up to 10 inches long. It blooms from September to December. It requires: low light intensity, high humidity, and a temperature of 50° to 55°. This species can be grown outdoors under lath until frost, after which it should be moved indoors. After bloom give very little water until growth resumes the following spring.

Phalaenopsis

This graceful orchid frequently called the moth orchid, has 4 to 8 thick leathery spatula-shaped leaves that droop over the side of the pot. Its 6 to 8 large snowy-white or pinkish-lavender flowers open anytime from January to May depending on variety.

Phalaenopsis like it warm, not below 60° to 65° at night. They require excellent drainage, high humidity. Keep plants moist, but not saturated, at all times.

Laelia   *Oncidium*   *Odontoglossum*   *Phalaenopsis*

HOW TO GROW ORCHIDS

Potting medium

Orchids fall into two classifications: *epiphytic*—includes cattleyas, dendrobiums, and odontoglossums, all of which grow in branches of trees; *terrestial*—includes cypripediums, which grow in soil under trees. Grow epiphytic orchids in osmunda fiber, or in one of the new tree bark products now being sold for orchid potting mix; and terrestial orchids in a loose potting soil such as 2 parts soil, 1 part shredded osmunda fiber, 1 part leaf mold, and 1 part sand.

Light intensity

Light intensity for orchids generally should be cut to about 80 per cent of the outside light—dark enough so you can just barely see a shadow. More sunlight than this is apt to burn the foliage. Inside the house the light behind sheer curtains in an east window is satisfactory for plants requiring high light intensity. (Dendrobiums require slightly more light than this and may be best in a southern exposure if the light is filtered.)

A look at the cattleya orchid's foliage will tell you immediately whether the plant is happy in its location. If the room is too dark, leaves will be dark green; if light is too strong, leaves will be yellow-green. When the light is right, foliage is apple green.

Humidity

One of the easiest ways to maintain high humidity in the house is to place pots on a pan of gravel half filled with water. This will not be enough water to wet the pots, but it will provide a constant source of humidity in the air surrounding the plants. Placing wet sponges among the pots is also an effective way of maintaining humidity.

Water

When the potting medium looks dry and the pot feels light when lifted, the plant needs water. Epiphytic or-

chids such as the cattleya, which store water in their pseudo-bulbs to carry them through dry periods in their native habitat, require less water than terrestial forms. Terrestial orchids, such as cypripedium, have no place to store water and require more frequent watering.

Overwatering is the main cause of failure with orchids. When orchids receive too much moisture, their oxygen supply is cut off and rot sets in. The leaves and pseudo-bulbs shrivel, and the amateur may feel that his plants are suffering from lack of water, when quite the reverse is true.

It's difficult to work out a definite rule for watering. It's safe to say: water when the growing medium is *almost* dry. You can determine this by lifting the pot to judge its weight, or by rapping its side sharply. If

Black metal pans are filled with white granite pebbles and water to provide the humidity necessary for growing orchids in the warm, dry atmosphere of the house.

there is a ringing sound instead of a dull one, the plant needs water.

Repotting

Most orchids require repotting every two years, and orchids suffer shock and setback if they are not divided at the right time. The best time to repot is when the new roots start to grow. Generally, this is shortly after flowering and can be detected when the live eye at the base of the most recent pseudo-bulb begins to swell. Be sure to repot before the potting medium becomes decomposed, soggy, and moss-covered. Orchids often take two to three years to recover from growing in an exhausted medium.

To remove the plant from its old container, pass a long knife around the inside of the pot to loosen, and pry it out, using a screw driver or similar instrument as a wedge. Remove as much as possible of the old, rotted compost from the roots, and cut off any dead or broken roots. If division is needed, do so at repotting time. In any case, it is a good idea to remove any badly shriveled back bulbs.

Select a new pot that is very porous and large enough to accommodate two years' growth. You can estimate the size needed by gauging the amount of growth your plant made in the past couple of years. Overpotting, or placing a plant in a pot too large, is dangerous since it encourages overwatering.

Enlarge the drainage hole in the bottom of the pot to an inch in diameter by gently hammering the edges. This permits better drainage and provides more air circulation for the epiphytic roots. Fill the bottom third of the pot with clean broken crock, being careful not to block the hole.

In most areas, bark mixtures are rapidly replacing osmunda fiber as a potting medium for orchids because they are more readily available, less expensive, and easier to handle.

To repot an orchid, first fill in the voids in the root ball with the potting medium which has been slightly dampened beforehand. Set the plant in the pot so that the rhizome is $\frac{1}{3}$ inch below the rim of the pot, with the back of the rhizome as close as possible to the side of the pot. Fill in around the root ball with the potting medium and use a blunt stick or thumb and forefinger to firm it toward the center of the pot. Tamping the pot on the bench or other hard surface as you work will help further to settle the potting medium around the plant. Firm potting is important, especially with cattleya orchids.

After potting, water the plant daily for 3 days. (Watering also helps to settle the potting mixture around the plant.) After this period, water once every 3 or 4 days, depending on your climate or the temperature in your house. There is little danger of overwatering orchids potted in bark mixtures because they are so porous that water drains through very readily.

Sprinkling the leaves of orchids lightly after potting is beneficial in warm inland areas, but be sure to sprinkle early in the morning so that leaves will be completely dry by evening.

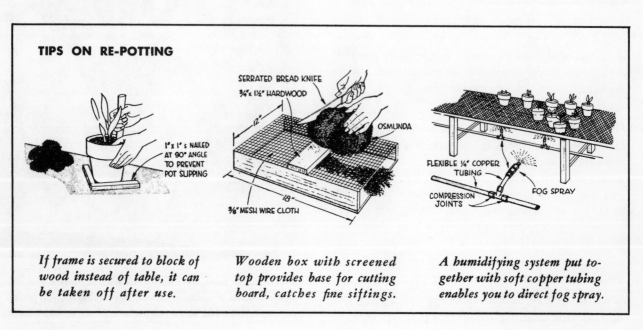

TIPS ON RE-POTTING

If frame is secured to block of wood instead of table, it can be taken off after use.

Wooden box with screened top provides base for cutting board, catches fine siftings.

A humidifying system put together with soft copper tubing enables you to direct fog spray.

Monstera deliciosa (also sold as P. pertusum*).*
Mature foliage, to three feet, perforated with
holes on either side of midrib. Use limited to
large room or entryway. Magnificent effect here:
plant is trained up moss pole between
fir posts that support the roof.

PHILODENDRON: TOP FAVORITE AMONG THE INDOOR FOLIAGE PLANTS

The philodendron is almost a stock item in thousands of homes. So it seems, at least, from the number of plants sold in nurseries, florist shops, department stores, and supermarkets.

Here are the questions most frequently asked by people who grow philodendrons—and our answers:

How often should philodendrons be repotted, and what is the best potting mix for them? Philodendrons do not have a very large root system, so shouldn't need repotting more frequently than once every 2 or 3 years. For fuller, more lush growth all the way to the base, set several plants together in one pot. Use a loose, well drained soil mix. (See section on potting mixes.)

Why does growth on a philodendron become weak and floppy? Such weak growth is frequently due to lack of light. Philodendrons like strong light, but should never be exposed to the direct rays of the sun immediately behind glass. Solid glass windows become very hot and often burn soft growth quite close to them. Set plants back at least 3 feet from glass not screened by blinds or thin draperies.

What causes black spots on the leaves? Black spots in the center of the leaf may mean your plant is getting too much water. Philodendrons like a moderately moist but well drained soil. Large plants usually require a good soaking once a week. Apply water until it runs through the pot into the saucer. Pour off any water that remains in the saucer 2 to 3 hours after watering the plant.

ROOT-PRUNING A PHILODENDRON. *1. Tangled mass of surface roots on the top of the pot looks unsightly. Roots may be four feet long. This is a non-climber.*

2. Carefully pull out and straighten as many roots as you can. Don't pull roots if they are firmly embedded in the soil. Cut several of them back to about six inches.

An accumulation of salts in the soil may also cause spotting of foliage. Salts build up in the soil when water drains through it too slowly. Be sure all watering has a flushing, leaching effect.

What causes leaves to brown and dry on the edges? This browning and drying may be due to an accumulation of salts in the potting medium; to overwatering; or more likely, to underwatering. Small plants require more frequent watering. When the surface dries out it is time to water. To avoid excess evaporation from small pots, mulch the surface of the soil with pebbles.

Why do leaves of the split-leaf philodendron and the monstera stop splitting? Several factors may effect the splitting of leaves: lack of light, soggy soil, lack of fertilizer. The first two factors are discussed above. Fertilize plants once every 4 to 6 weeks to keep them in good growth. Use a liquid fertilizer or one of the water-soluble dry fertilizers sold for use on house plants.

The method by which plants are propagated has an influence on the degree of splitting, too. Plants propagated from stem cuttings may have to form 5 or 6 leaves before they split. This is particularly true of cuttings taken from lateral growth or mature wood well back from the growing tip. Plants propagated from seed may take an undetermined length of time before they develop split leaves.

Can long aerial roots, hanging down from the stem, be cut off? It is probably best not to take off aerial roots, for even in the home these appendages serve a purpose. Since they help to supply oxygen to the plant, retaining the aerial roots may help overcome poor drainage conditions. Roots hanging down over the side of the pot can be bent up and tucked down into the soil.

Is it unusual for the split leaf philodendrons to flower? Will they set seed? It is not unusual for these plants to flower, but they usually require a high humidity and lots of warmth in order to do so. In mild winter climates, the monstera develops quite palatable fruit.

What is the best way to clean philodendron foliage? It's a good idea to remove dust from leaves of foliage plants about once a month. Use mild soap and water or skimmed milk. If you want to give them a high polish, use some of the commercial cleaners or polishes. Never use oil. Water the plants the day before you clean them to avoid leaf burn when you use one of the commercial polishes.

Once in a while on a warm day, it is beneficial to move large plants outdoors into a shady spot and hose them off. Allow them to drip fairly dry before moving them back into the house. Never take a house plant outdoors, however, when the air is much colder outside than in.

What can be done to philodendrons when they become too tall? When plants get too large, propagate

3. Push root stumps down into the soil. Add more fresh soil, and mound over with pea gravel to keep the roots cool and aerated. Lay uncut roots on surface.

4. Aerial surface roots are characteristic of philodendrons. Here, three are left on the top. Water well with a hormone solution after you transplant or root-prune.

new plants from cuttings. The small vining types can easily be rooted in water. Take cuttings 3 to 5 leaves long.

Increase the larger split-leaf philodendrons and the monstera by making cuttings or by air-layering. With these larger-leafed plants, proportionately shorter cuttings

—2 to 3 leaf joints long—are best. Root them in a mixture of half sand and half peat moss. Keep moist.

To induce double or triple crowns on the self-headed or tree-type philodendrons, cut out the growing tip of the plant.

Varieties of philodendron

Often sold as P. cruentum, *but identity is disputed. Soft growth. Back sides of young leaves are red-brown.*

P. radiatum *(offered as* P. dubium*). Deeply cut, almost star-shaped leaf. Takes more light than most.*

P. hastatum. *Dark jade green leaves shaped like large arrowheads. Good for training on totem poles in pots.*

P. oxycardium *(sold as P. cordatum).* *Most common. Small heart-shaped leaves. Grows in water or soil.*

P. laciniatum. *Dark leathery leaf similar to P. panduraeforme. Retains leaves with age. Lanky in dark.*

P. panduraeforme. *Large fiddle shaped leaf. Retains lower foliage with age. Becomes lanky in dark.*

P. squamiferum. *Large five-lobed leaf shaped like a ship's anchor. Red scales along the petioles.*

P. sodiroi. *Variegated species. Foliage shades of olive green and gray which give a silvery sheen.*

P. wendlandii. *Forms compact rosette of spatulate leaves. Does not vine. Tolerant of heat, humidity.*

Two varieties—*P.* São Paulo, a variety of *P. selloum* and *P.* Eichleri—were introduced into the trade in the spring of 1956. The variety São Paulo is self-heading and it has a much darker green leaf, with margins that are more frilled, and more upright stems. The vigor of this plant becomes evident quite soon after planting out. Give it plenty of room in containers or planters.

Frilled leaf is a notable feature of the *Philodendron* São Paulo.

Larger, with narrower leaves, is variety *P. Eichleri,* a king-size version of *P. selloum.* In coastal areas the long, flat, arrow-shaped leaves have been especially resistant to sun. Low temperatures in those areas have not harmed the plants.

The cultural requirements of these varieties are quite simple. Use a light, porous soil mixture. These plants are heavy feeders and respond quickly to fertilizing with a balanced fertilizer.

The self-heading nature of these plants causes each to form a neat and compact crown of leaves that is much more manageable than the vine-like stems of some species of philodendrons.

Most of the new hybrids will stand temperatures to 32°. Some have withstood lower temperatures.

HOME-MADE CONTAINERS:

On the following pages are plans for a variety of plant containers that you can build yourself. The finished boxes are shown in the photographs.

Size and shape. It is usually best to make the box the size and shape to fit the place you want to put it. Plants adapt themselves very well to the box they are in. You can grow almost any plant in a box measuring 2 feet square and 2 feet tall. It is a good idea to put deep-rooted plants in taller, narrower containers, and shallow rooted plants in lower, wider ones.

Another limitation on the size of the container is its weight after it is filled with soil. A cubic foot of soil weighs from 70 to 90 pounds. A box 2 feet square and 2 feet tall will weigh from 550 to 750 pounds when it is planted.

MATERIALS TO USE

Wood is the most popular material for large plant containers. It is durable, easy to build with, and looks at home in a garden. Wood containers will last longer if the joints are treated with white lead, if corners are screwed and glued, and if the inside is waterproofed. You can seal the inside of a box with a coating of asphalt, neoprene, or tree seal, or use a liner of 20-gage galvanized iron. Staining or painting is optional in most cases.

Redwood and *cedar* are widely used for plant boxes because they resist rot, and both weather beautifully with little or no outside finish.

Douglas fir is stronger than redwood or cedar. Its strength is an advantage for a large box. When treated with a preservative, Douglas fir will resist decay for many years. The outside of the box can be treated with stain to keep it from turning dark.

Pine can also be used. It is soft and very easy to work. It is best to use two-inch material for a big plant box. Pine, like Douglas fir, should be treated with a preservative.

Exterior plywood has the advantage of light weight and great strength. However, a plant box of plywood calls for careful construction. Seal all edges and joints as you build it. Put a cap on the top edge and seal the inside before planting. The outside of the box should be painted and will require periodic refinishing.

Lightweight aggregates like pumice, expanded mica, or shale, can be used with cement to make handsome large-scale plant containers. However, success with the design and construction of these containers usually calls for a pretty thorough working knowledge of concrete.

• • •

This flare-sided container makes an ideal setting for a miniature garden. Plants will grow happily in it and remain in scale for a long time. Construction calls for compound miters at the corners and use of 1-inch redwood or cedar. Base and beveled top give box an attractive finish. Best planted where it will remain—heavy and awkward to move around.

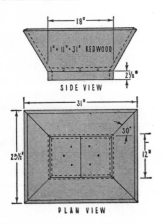

Plant with *a tree or shub, plus a few perennials and a ground cover or some bulbs for miniature box garden.*

These little planters will work perfectly well for bonsai, as well as for the little plants shown here.

All the containers are 1-inch rough redwood stock. Butt joints are fastened with dowels to prevent metal stains on the sides. The bottoms and feet are nailed on, since stains underneath won't show.

To bring out the grain, burn the redwood with a blowtorch, and remove the charred wood with a wire brush. (Although photographs show the burning and wire brushing of a finished box, we later found it easier to do these jobs before the parts were assembled.)

The containers are attractive without any special finish, though you may prefer to darken the wood with a stain. A combination of beeswax, turpentine, and linseed oil gives a dark, waxy finish. You should coat the inside with a commercial wood preservative to prevent rot.

For planters like these, *look for neglected plants because they often have interesting shapes. Plants are Meyer lemon, upper left; Arctostaphylos uva-ursi, top; deodar cedar and Irish moss, top right; azalea, Irish moss, and cushion, dianthus, center; nandina, lower right. Creek rocks add texture interest, blend with combed wood*

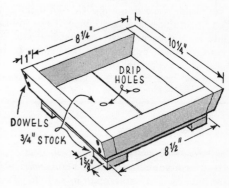

Blowtorch *burns soft portions of the wood, doesn't effect the hard grain. You don't need to burn inside as soil will cover*

Wire brush *removes charred parts. If the end grain is unattractive, you can make the planters with mitered corner joints*

Dimensions *are given for planter in upper right of photograph. You can use this method to construct most any size planter*

These containers merit more than usual attention because of their clean, simple design, elegant proportions, and fine craftsmanship. They are handsome pieces in themselves, and are ideally compatible with plants.

Georg Hoy, who designed these boxes, burned out the soft wood with a blowtorch, then removed the charred portions with a wire brush. Containers were fastened with wooden dowels and pegs instead of nails. The outside of each container was finished with a preparation that contained beeswax, turpentine, and linseed oil; inside was coated with a commercial paint that prevents leaking and rot. Container on left is 10 by 14 inches; smaller box on right is 6¼ by 10 inches.

Here is a plant box extremely simple to put together. Once you have the basic container, you can do all sorts of things to vary its design.

When assembled you have a box 12 inches deep with 14 by 14-inch outside dimensions. Bore ½-inch holes in the bottom for drainage.

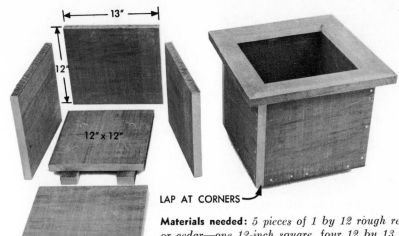

Or paint box black, then nail 1 by 1-inch wood strips around box, lapping them as you did sides. Strips painted gray

LAP AT CORNERS

Materials needed: *5 pieces of 1 by 12 rough redwood or cedar—one 12-inch square, four 12 by 13 inches; 1 by 3-inch surfaced stock for cap; 1 by 1 cleats or 2-inch squares for feet; and 12-penny galvanized nails*

Aluminum and wood *give an interesting contrast. One-inch aluminum angle strips are fastened to corners of box with brads*

Wooden corners *may also be used to dress up the box. Redwood or cedar exterior molding works very well for this variation*

Lath batten *(½ by 1 inch), nailed vertically around the box, provides still another variation for this basic container*

Sometimes it is easier and cheaper to make a decorative box than a plain one. If a plain box is to look handsome year after year, it must be of the best grade of lumber and perfect in construction detail. Box corners should be mitered rather than square cut.

Here 1 by 2-inch pieces hide a box made from an inexpensive grade of 2-inch redwood nailed together in the simplest fashion.

Designed by Landscape Architects Osmundson & Staley.

THEODORE OSMUNDSON

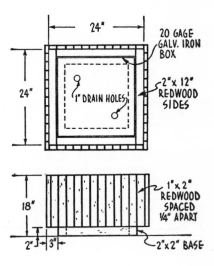

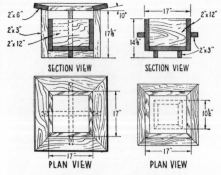

Cleats, which keep this planter at left above the ground, match the header boards in the paving and continue up the sides of the planter to support the top rail and provide a strong design element. The planter at the right has a 2-by-6 rail midway up the side of the box. Both planters were designed by Landscape Architect Kathryn Stedman.

The team of Osmundson & Staley designed this plant box, similar to the one pictured above. It has held its own through several years of experimentation with other designs.

The landscape architects, striving for long-lasting beauty, specify a clear grade of redwood. Inside metal liners will prevent the wood from staining, and a coating a clear plastic (polyester) available in hobby and boat shops will give permanent protection to the outside.

THEODORE OSMUNDSON

Sturdiness *is all-important. Though 1-inch lumber will hold soil adequately, warping follows and destroys clean appearance*

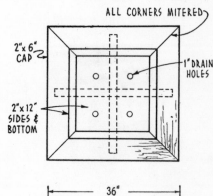

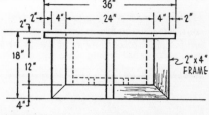

Rough sawn cedar, left to weather naturally, was used to make these two plant boxes designed by Venning Hollis of Seattle.

Box *planted with Japanese maple. Built of ¾-inch-thick cedar, with 1 by 2-inch cedar strips nailed around the outside*

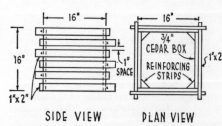

As sketch shows, *corners of plant box are reinforced by triangular strips of wood*

•••

Outstanding features of this box, aside from its appearance, are its exceptional strength and heat resistance. Sides are thicker than on most wooden boxes, and the protruding pieces partially shade the sides. Baronian and Danielson, landscape architects in Davis, California, designed and built the box. Its insulating qualities suit it to areas with very hot summers.

The boards were put together with galvanized nails of varying sizes: from 2-penny for the ¼-inch boards up to 30-penny for the 3-inch boards. The latter were pre-drilled before nailing. The bottom is a piece of plywood with holes drilled for drainage. It stands on a square frame of mitered 2 by 3's.

The bottom piece of plywood was treated with creosote to make it last longer.

R. DANIELSON

This container's *sides are made of scrap redwood nailed together as shown below. Plant is variegated* Euonymus japonicus

Bottom and inside *surfaces were lined up even, tops sawed off afterward. You could saw all pieces same length before nailing*

•••

The simple, rugged character of this box makes it an ideal container for a strong, picturesque plant. It is beautifully scaled to the curving black pine *(Pinus thunbergii)* you see here.

Actually, there are two boxes—an inner one of 1-inch material holds the plant; the outer box, purely decorative, is made of 3 by 4's toenailed together at the corners.

The pine is planted in a mixture of 2 parts soil, 1 part sharp gravel, 1 part leaf mold, and 1 part peat moss. There are drainage holes in the inside box.

This tree has been allowed to grow naturally without pruning, except for one pinching of the main leader.

Other plants that would look at home in this box are magnolia, loquat, rice paper plant *(Tetrapanax papyrifera)*, and *Fatsia japonica.*

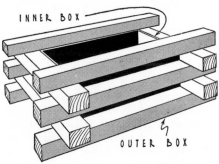

First, build liner *holding plant; place 3 by 4's around it, toenail corners. Dimensions: 24¾ by 31 by 13 inches deep*

Interesting shape *of Japanese black pine makes a handsome display against background formed by opaque glass screen*

WILLIAM APLIN

•••

Heavy trim around plant boxes gives strong shadow pattern. Landscape architects: Osmundson & Staley.

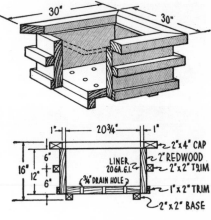

These small planters *hold (left to right) marguerites, New Zealand flax, and showy sedum*

ROBERT COX

• • •

With a table saw and dado attachments, you can easily make any one of the planters shown above in an afternoon. Chances are you'll want at least three, because planters this size work best in groups. We've limited the sawing to a minimum number of settings, so you can readily mass produce these containers.

This project, incidentally, is a good one for teaching a boy how to work with a power saw.

Approximately five gallons in size, each of the containers shown here is light enough, even when full of soil, to be moved without the aid of rollers. Thus, you can easily move the plant for a change of scene, to take advantage of seasonal blossoms, or to experiment with sun and shade conditions to find where it thrives best. A small planter also works well as a temporary, decorative resting place for plants in pots or cans.

You can save money if you use scrap lumber. Ask your lumber dealer for "shorts," such as roofing cut-offs. These odd pieces usually cost considerably less than standard lengths.

• • •

The construction method calls for interlocking strips that resemble square "logs." First, cut the stock to the desired length (these were 15½ inches long). Width isn't important since the stock will be ripped into thin strips. For greatest strength have the long dimension *with* the grain of the wood.

Notch the stock with dadoes 1 inch from each end on both sides. Dadoes are ¾ inch wide and ⅜ inch deep. If they are too shallow, there will be gaps between the strips when you assemble the planter. Once the dadoes are cut, rip the stock into ¾-inch strips and assemble as shown.

This planter *requires four half-size strips to fill the gaps at the top and bottom*

After notching *with dado, rip the lumber into ¾-inch strips. Be sure to use a push stick for safety on the narrow cuts*

R. J. DE CRISTOFORO

Assemble parts *like log cabin, using a waterproof glue between each section. Nail the corners after every third strip*

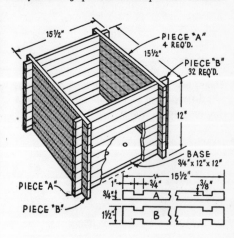

R. J. DE CRISTOFORO

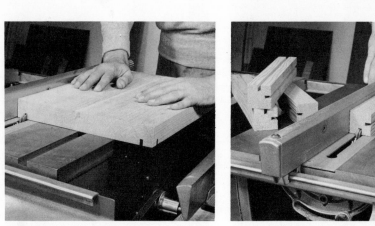

After base is cut, *form dadoes parallel to the four sides. Hold stock flat on table so that dadoes will be uniform in depth*

Dadoes *in corner posts are cut at same setting as base (¼″ wide, ½″ deep). Cut dadoes on two adjacent sides of the stock*

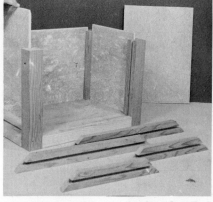

When corner posts *are glued and nailed, slide in all the panels. Then add the top frame, and nail securely into corner posts*

● ● ●

First step is to cut the base, corner posts, and top frame to the size shown in the sketch. Next, set your dado for a ¼-inch width, and cut all tne required grooves. If you use a shim between the outside blades of the dado, the side panels will slide in the grooves without binding.

After dadoes are done, cut a notch in each corner of the base to accommodate the corner posts. Fasten posts and slide in side panels. Those shown are asbestos cement board but tempered hardboard or exterior plywood can also be used.

This planter is heaviest of the three. You can paint panels or leave them exposed

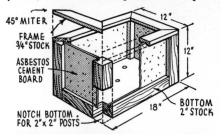

● ● ●

By bevel cutting both sides of identical pieces of stock, you can create a round planter of any size. Again, the first step is to cut the stock to length. Use a hollow ground blade, or sand pieces smooth after cutting with regular blade. Sand carefully or you'll throw off the circle.

Tilt the saw blade (or the table if you have a tilt-table saw) to exactly 7½°. Be accurate because a slight error will be multiplied 48 times. It's wise to make a trial cut in scrap wood first and check the angle with a protractor.

Lock the rip fence for your initial bevel along one edge. Then reset the fence to cut 24 two-inch segments. Run each strip through a second time to bevel the other side. Assemble segments with two staples at each end. If you own a stapling gun you can use it to speed up the job, but be sure the staples are galvanized so they won't rust in wet weather and stain your planter.

Use the assembled circle as a template to draw the outline of the base. We used aluminum for the outside bands, but brass, stainless steel, or plastic clothesline will work just as well.

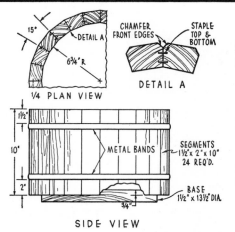

Round planter *demands precise sawing. Chamfer front edges for shadow effect*

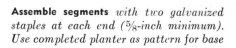

SIDE VIEW

All three planters are tight enough to hold soil, but if you wish, you can line the insides with roofing paper or felt. Drill drain holes through planter bottoms after the paper is in place.

Assemble segments *with two galvanized staples at each end (⅝-inch minimum). Use completed planter as pattern for base*

Set blade *at exactly 7½°. Set fence so the pieces measure 2 inches across top. Use smooth-cutting blade to insure a snug fit*

HOME-MADE CONTAINERS   107

This container grows with the plant. A tapered wood box forms the base. A second box is nested in this and held with dowels. The top unit is a separate lip. Compound miters make building this container a real challenge. The plant is a *Rhododendron rutherfordianum.*

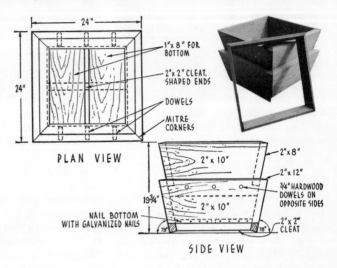

BLAIR STAPP

Take-apart box is for plants you want to root prune or take out of box later. The cap lifts off, and asbestos board sides pull out of grooves in ends. Easy to make, this container requires only dado cuts for the box and miter cuts for the top. The ends are wire-brushed for texture. Tree is Aleppo pine *(Pinus halepensis).*

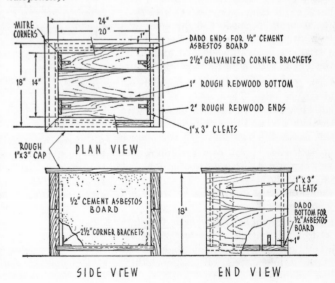

Planned for use with dwarf citrus, this plywood box is painted tangerine color and has brass trim to cover plywood edges. The frame is made of 2 by 2's. Box is screwed and glued on three sides; fourth side can be unscrewed to remove plant.

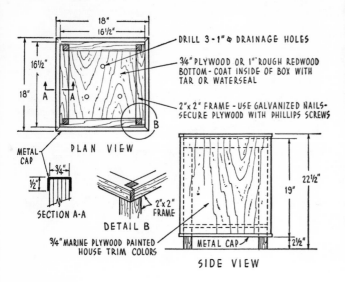

PLAN VIEW

DRILL 3 - 1" ⌀ DRAINAGE HOLES

¾" PLYWOOD OR 1" ROUGH REDWOOD BOTTOM - COAT INSIDE OF BOX WITH TAR OR WATERSEAL

2" x 2" FRAME - USE GALVANIZED NAILS - SECURE PLYWOOD WITH PHILLIPS SCREWS

METAL CAP

SECTION A-A

DETAIL B

2" x 2" FRAME

¾" MARINE PLYWOOD PAINTED HOUSE TRIM COLORS

METAL CAP

SIDE VIEW

This plant box is inexpensive and easy to make with hand tools. It requires only a minimum of cutting and joining. Use rough redwood, a 1 by 8-inch board 14 feet long. (This length allows for a little waste so you can trim out knots.) Cut 4 pieces 14 inches long for the ends and 6 pieces 16 inches long for the sides and bottom. Be sure annual rings in the wood curve as is shown in sketch, so shrinkage will pull the edges of each board inward. Cleats on bottom raise box to allow for drainage.

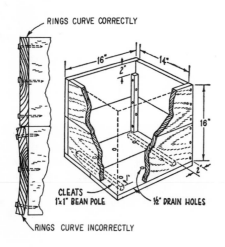

RINGS CURVE CORRECTLY

RINGS CURVE INCORRECTLY

CLEATS 1" x 1" BEAN POLE

½" DRAIN HOLES

Brick sized holders. *Recessed base keeps foreground block from looking bricklike*

Small potted plants *are staged in larger, more stable units. In the larger one, haydite creates a lightweight aggregate; in others, beach pebbles produce contrasting texture*

Many variations *possible: integral color in the mix, applied stain, or a terrazzo finish*

• • •

Which comes first, the container or the plant? Some people collect plants and look for ways to display them; some collect containers and look for plants to fill them.

The plants and containers shown here should more than satisfy both motives. They are the work of Landscape Architect John Carmack.

Scores of interesting plants are available in 2-inch pots for the dish garden enthusiast. If they're displayed as potted plants, singly or in collection, the clay pots seem dinky and temporary. But placed within larger, more stable units, the pots are no longer distracting and the plants become all-important.

Not only do these containers transform an ordinary plant into a growing gem, but they also keep it in good health by holding moisture around the pot.

How to make the concrete containers . . .

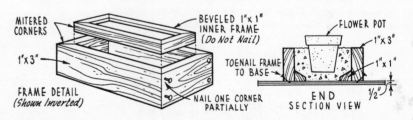

Frames: To keep wood from absorbing water from mix and to prevent sticking, soak frame in motor oil overnight.

Mix: Use fairly stiff mix, 3 parts cement, 1 of sand, 2 of pebbles or pumice.

Procedure: Presoak pot in water. Pour frame about half full of mix; twist pot into position, and fill in concrete to top of frame. Twist pot frequently to prevent sticking and to insure a smooth inner finish. After the concrete firms, brush lightly to expose aggregate. A day later, strip off form and twist out pot. Run water over aggregate surface. After concrete is hard, scrub it with a wire brush.

• • •

To make concrete planter, use two cardboard cartons. One should be enough smaller to leave about 1½ to 2 inches of space at the bottom and on all four sides when placed inside the other. Make concrete mix of 1 part cement, 1 part sand, 1½ to 2 parts vermiculite or other lightweight aggregate. Stir dry ingredients together and then add only enough water to make a thick, grainy mush. Mix well and pour about a 1½ to 2-inch layer in the bottom of the larger carton. Tamp down the mix, then place the small carton inside, weighting it down with several bricks or rocks. Pour and tamp the mix between the two cartons to form side walls of planter.

After concrete has set for 12 hours or more, remove cardboard forms. Let the concrete dry slowly for several days, then shape the planter, using chiseling and rasping tools. For the preliminary work, use an ordinary cold chisel and hammer. Finally, rasp, then wirebrush the surface. Before you fill the planter with soil, cure it by letting it stand three or four days with several changes of water.

• • •

Another easy-to-make planter is shown below. You need no complicated form— just a simple 1 by 6-inch frame and a box or block of wood the size of the opening. Place the frame and box or block on a pad of newspapers or a sheet of cardboard. Pour in the concrete mix, tamping it down into the side spaces until it is level with the top of the frame.

After the concrete has been leveled, set in place a 1-inch piece of wood into which you have driven several nails. The block of wood will be anchored to the concrete when it hardens and provide a base that will not scratch floors or furniture.

Simple frame and inside form for square planter may be oiled for easy removal

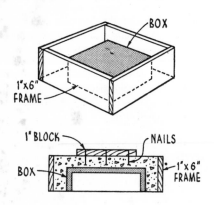

Concrete *container is easily made using wooden form. Could use hollow concrete block. Rush grows here in woodland pool*

BLAIR STAPP

Exposed aggregate *finish on small planter achieved with wire brush after concrete sets overnight. Designer: George Homsey*

ROBERT COX

A wonderful window into a tropical world, this plant terrarium has its own climate, linked to the outside only by ventilation holes (drilled after this photograph was taken) to release any heat generated by the light inside. It needs little water or care

● ● ●

There's an appeal for all ages in this terrarium. For a child, it's a miniature garden that he can watch grow and change. For an adult it can be an incubator to give house plants as good a start as they would get in a greenhouse. It's especially attractive at night when the room lights are off and the light in the lid casts a soft glow on the plants.

The materials for the terrarium cost $16; the plants cost $10. Construction and planting took about 10 hours.

MATERIALS AND CONSTRUCTION

The terrarium is 17½ inches square and 19¾ inches high. Here is the list of materials and a cutting guide:

Glass—4 panes, 15 15/16 inches square.

¾-inch plywood—a 16-inch square (for the bottom).

¼-inch plywood—a 17½-inch square (for the top).

¼-inch quarter round—43 feet (cut into 32 pieces 16 inches long).

¾-inch square stock—5½ feet, cut into four 18¾-inch lengths for corner posts, four 16-inch lengths for framing the top, and four 17½-inch lengths for the lid.

1 by 2-inch stock—5½ feet, cut into four 16-inch lengths for framing the bottom.

⅜ by 1⅛-inch molding—5½ feet, cut into four 16-inch lengths for guide rails.

Lumiline tube (40 watts, 12 inches long, white) with sockets and receptacles.

Stain, glue, brads, small turn switch, 8 feet of electrical cord, male plug.

Don't frame the glass too tightly; allow about 1/16 inch on all sides for expansion. Measure the glass carefully and adjust the frame measurements if the panes were not cut too accurately.

See the sketch for the construction. Here is the how-to-do-it sequence: Stain all pieces first. Then glue and nail horizontal framing to the bottom piece. Drill a ½-inch drain hole. Fasten corner posts in

place and add the top horizontal framing. Measure the diagonals on each side; they should be equal if the frame is square.

Next, put in all inside quarter rounds with glue and brads. Put the glass panes in place, securing them with a temporary brad at each side. Fasten top and bottom outside quarter rounds, remove temporary brads, and fasten side pieces.

Check top measurements before you make the lid. Drill ventilation holes. Glue the ¾-inch stock around the lower edges of the top, then place molding strips on edge inside the framing. Use cardboard shims between the framing and the guide rails so the lid won't fit too tightly.

Bolt the lumiline tube to the lid and wire the cord to it. Drill a hole for the turn switch in one corner of the lid and wire to one of the electric wires. Fasten the cord to the lid with small staples. The lid shown here is loose so it can be lifted off. Paint the inside of the bottom with a commercial rot preventive. Plug the drain hole with a cork.

PLANTING

Air in a terrarium stays humid, as in a greenhouse, so the climate is ideal for a variety of house plants, tropicals, and semi-tropicals. Choose young, slow-growing plants that won't soon crowd one another.

Shops that specialize in house plants are the best place to look. You can often find seedling-sized house plants in variety stores.

Leave the plants in their pots. This will limit their growth and allow you to move them around, or thin them without disrupting the whole planting.

Place the largest plants first, then add some sponge-rock. (This is sold in nurseries for about $1 a cubic foot—the amount we used. It keeps the terrarium humid by holding water for a long time.) Then arrange the smaller plants and cover the pots with sponge-rock—just up to, but not covering, the base of the stems. Wet the plants and the sponge-rock. After several hours, drain off any excess water through the drain hole. Water condensation on the glass each night will indicate moisture inside. Don't water again until the sponge-rock feels almost dry; this may not be for several months.

These are the plants in the terrarium: palm (*Chamaedorea elegans,* also listed as *Neanthe bella*), Velvet plant (Gynura aurantiaca), Australian cliff brake (*Pellaea falcata*), *Peperomia fraseri* (sometimes sold as *P. resediflora*), *P. rubella,* Hart's tongue fern (*Phyllitis scolopendrium,* sometimes sold as *Scolopendrium vulgare),* two species of club moss (selaginella), and syngonium Ysidro.

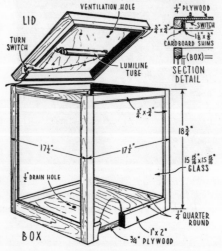

This sketch *shows construction details of box. Note the drain and ventilation holes, which are necessary if the lid fits tight*